Teaching About Climate Change

Cool Schools Tackle Global Warming

Edited by
Tim Grant and Gail Littlejohn

NEW SOCIETY PUBLISHERS

Green Teacher

Cataloging in Publication Data:
A catalog record for this publication is available from the National Library of Canada.

Cover design by Diane McIntosh.
Design and production by Green Living Editorial & Design Services.

Printed in Canada on acid-free, partially recycled (20 percent post-consumer) paper using soy-based inks by Transcontinental/Best Book Manufacturers.

Green Teacher acknowledges the support of the Government of Canada's Climate Change Action Fund.

Canada

New Society Publishers acknowledges the support of the Government of Canada through the Book Publishing Industry Development Program (BPIDP) for our publishing activities, and the assistance of the Province of British Columbia through the British Columbia Arts Council.

BRITISH
COLUMBIA
ARTS COUNCIL
Supported by the Province of British Columbia

Paperback ISBN: 0-86571-437-1

Inquiries regarding requests to reprint all or part of *Teaching About Climate Change* should be addressed to New Society Publishers at the address below.

To order directly from the publishers, please add $4.50 shipping to the price of the first copy, and $1.00 for each additional copy (plus GST in Canada). Send check or money order to:

Green Teacher
95 Robert Street, Toronto, ON M5S 2K5, Canada
P.O. Box 1431, Lewiston, NY 14092, USA
or
New Society Publishers
P.O. Box 189, Gabriola Island, BC V0R 1X0, Canada

New Society Publishers aims to publish books for fundamental social change through non-violent action. We focus especially on sustainable living, progressive leadership, and educational and parenting resources. Our full list of books can be browsed on the worldwide web at: www.newsociety.com

NEW SOCIETY PUBLISHERS
www.newsociety.com

Table of Contents

Acknowledgements

This book reflects the inspired efforts of a great many individuals who share a common goal of finding a more sustainable way of living on the planet. We especially thank the many contributing authors who in these pages share their expertise and their passion for learning experiences that will help prepare young people for the challenges that lie ahead. All gave freely of their time and worked hard to meet deadlines in the midst of their own busy schedules.

We are also grateful to the Government of Canada's Climate Change Action Fund which supported the production of this book in both English and French and its distribution to schools across Canada. This federal program has funded dozens of educational projects and teachers' workshops in Canada and is a wonderful example of how much can be accomplished on a modest budget. We could not have published this book without the Fund's support and we owe a special thanks to Ann Jarnet for her encouragement and guidance over the past two years.

Much gratitude is also due to Isabelle Morin, Marcel Lafleur and Jean Robitaille, our partners in this project at ERE Éducation in Québec City. They assisted in developing the contents of the book and provided much helpful advice over the past 18 months as they prepared the French edition. Their flexibility, good humor and patience with our foibles — linguistic and otherwise — was greatly appreciated.

In the challenging task of sifting and selecting learning resources for the listings in the Organizations and Resources section, we were fortunate to be able to draw on the experience of a number of educators who are already teaching about climate change and fossil-fuel alternatives such as renewable energy and transportation options. The following experts shared with us their favorite curricula and learning resources: in Canada, Andrew Casey (NS), Cheryl Lepatski (AB), David Lunn (AB), Geoff Peach (ON), and Kathy Worobec (AB); in the United States, Glenda Abney (MO), Carl Bollwinkel (IA), Merrilee Harrigan (VA), Jennie Lane (WI), Chris Mason (MA), Karen Reagor (KY), Susan Schleith (FL), Blanche Scheinkopf (FL), Robert Vogl and Sonia Vogl (IL).

Finally, we want to express our sincere appreciation of the many other committed individuals who labored behind the scenes to make this book a reality: Lucy Segatti of Toronto who translated an article from French; Jennifer Adams at the Alliance for Saving Energy in Washington D.C. who provided instant answers to our queries about units of energy; the creative team of Tracy Kett and Brad Cundiff at Green Living in Toronto who developed the attractive page design and gave us many helpful suggestions; Chris Plant and friends at New Society Publishers on Gabriola Island who guided us in shaping the book; and our editorial assistant Lisa Newman, whose investigations uncovered many wonderful teaching resources of which we were previously unaware.

Tim Grant and Gail Littlejohn
Toronto

Introduction

by Tim Grant and Gail Littlejohn

There can be little doubt that climate change will be a significant issue, and possibly the central challenge to humankind, during the lifetime of today's students. In the past few decades, human activities have raised atmospheric concentrations of greenhouse gases to their highest level in 420,000 years, and a growing body of scientific research predicts rising temperatures and large scale alterations in weather patterns that will continue through the 21st century, even if we manage to curtail greenhouse gas emissions. Yet climate change is a phenomenon with which we humans have little experience, at least in historic times, and teaching about it presents special challenges to educators. The topic is complex because the Earth's systems are complex, and scientists themselves are not at all certain of the potential ramifications of our interference with these systems. Equally formidable from an educator's point of view is the intangibility of climate change: its global scale and seemingly slow progression make it a phenomenon that does not easily lend itself to classroom demonstration. And teachers and students who wish to take action on climate change find themselves up against the ingrained habits and attitudes of an industrial society created and powered by fossil fuels and supported by political inertia in establishing regulatory policies to curb greenhouse gas emissions.

Despite these obstacles, teaching about and taking action on climate change may not be as difficult as it seems. All it takes is a starting point. Accordingly, this book is intended as a primer to help teachers and students begin to explore some of the key questions related to climate change: What are its causes? What might we expect? What are governments doing about it? And, most important, what can schools and students do about it? In working with young people, teachers have a great many opportunities to address these vitally important questions. Many topics that would be part of a study of climate change are already part of most curricula: these include, for example, technology topics such as energy systems; social studies topics such as political decision-making; or geography and science topics such as weather systems, photosynthesis and decomposition, and adaptations of plants and animals to specific habitats and climatic conditions. Moreover, many teachers and students are already engaged in activities that are helping to reduce their own and their schools' greenhouse gas emissions: planting trees near the school building, replacing asphalt surfaces with native plant gardens, conserving energy and water, reducing waste, walking or cycling to school instead of driving. It is only a small step to incorporate discussion of climate change into these curricular areas and activities.

To help teachers find their own best starting point, the contributors to this book — all educators themselves — present a diverse array of learning activities for all age levels. Readers will find basic background information on the greenhouse effect and climate, accompanied by simple experiments that help students understand key concepts. As an aid in planning a unit or course of study, Milton McClaren and William Hammond outline a broad and balanced conceptual framework for climate change education which can be adapted for various grade levels. The core of the book, however, is activities that can be undertaken at school, at home and in the community to raise awareness and take action on reducing greenhouse gas emissions. Since transportation accounts for the largest portion of individual emissions, explorations of transportation alternatives figure prominently, but there are also ideas for investigating energy options and sustainable practices that would lessen our dependence on fossil fuels. Our aim throughout has been to suggest practical pathways into the topic of climate change, to invite teachers and students to examine the choices that lie ahead for us as a society, and to take action now in the belief that we cannot afford to wait until our politicians agree that it is time to do so.

A Climate of Change: The Context

As evidence of climate change mounts, it's time for the world's leaders — and teachers and students — to take action

by Louise Comeau and Dave Mussell

By the time today's high school graduates retire, the Earth's atmosphere could be loaded with three times more carbon dioxide than it had before the Industrial Revolution. Average surface temperatures around the globe could be from two to six degrees Celsius higher than present averages (and higher still at the poles). Low-lying islands and coastal populations could be at risk of submersion by rising seas. Extreme weather and climate calamities — droughts, severe storms, forest fires and floods — could be regular occurrences.[1]

But climate change is not just a problem of the future: there are clear signs that it is already here. Average global temperatures have increased by about 0.6° C in the past century, and the warming trend in Siberia, Canada's Arctic, and the Antarctic continent has been more than double that.[2] Glaciers are retreating, permafrost is melting, pack ice is thinning, and freeze-up is occurring later than normal. In the Arctic Ocean, sea ice is about 40 percent thinner during late summer and autumn than it was just a few decades ago, and the ice-free period is longer. Between 1885 and 1995, average sea level rose by 10 to 20 centimeters (4"-8"), mainly as a result of thermal expansion. It is expected to rise 50 centimeters (20") more by the year 2100 and to continue rising for centuries, even if global mean temperatures stabilize.[3]

These are the symptoms of a warming Earth as described by the growing body of research on climate change. In early 2001, the Intergovernmental Panel on Climate Change (IPCC) — the most systematic and broad-based scientific collaboration in history[4] — released its third assessment report, based on the research of more than 2,000 scientists from over

Photographs by Gail Littlejohn

130 countries. The IPCC's Summary for Policymakers declares unequivocally that "most of the warming observed over the last 50 years is attributable to human activities." Citing the 20th century's unprecedentedly rapid increase in greenhouse gases due to fossil fuel burning and deforestation, the IPCC reports that the present atmospheric concentration of carbon dioxide (CO_2) is the highest in 420,000 years and likely has not been exceeded during the past 20 million years.[5]

Among most governments, and indeed in most industry circles, there is no longer much doubt that climate change is a real issue. So strong is the scientific evidence that the IPCC's conclusions are virtually inescapable. Nonetheless, they represent a miracle of political compromise, arrived at only after months of intense pressure from oil-producing countries who continue to fight the suggestion that climate has already begun to change as a result of human activities. Political pressure to resist action on climate change is all too common, and those concerned about risks to health and the environment increasingly find themselves at odds with those who have an economic interest in the primary cause of the problem: the use of fossil fuels.

North America is not immune to these political pressures. For instance, in Canada, the surging Alberta economy is led by massive new oil sands projects in the Athabasca region. Newfoundland and Nova Scotia are headed in the same direction with the development of offshore oil and gas fields. This growth in fossil fuel production is matched by a rise in energy consumption. On a per capita basis, North Americans stand out from the rest of the world as the most profligate consumers of energy and emitters of greenhouse gases. Both Canada and the United States are characterized by comparatively low energy prices, highly energy-intensive industries, low efficiency standards, and cities built to encourage transportation in single-occupancy vehicles. As of 1996, Americans and Canadians, respectively, emitted an astounding 24.7 and 22.4 metric tonnes of CO_2 and CO_2-equivalents per capita, almost twice that of the average German and 80 times the average in India.[6]

At the 1992 United Nations Conference on Environment and Development (commonly known as the Rio Earth Summit), Canada and the United States were among more than 150 nations whose leaders signed the United Nations Framework Convention on Climate Change. In doing so, all of the parties agreed to work toward the Convention's main objective: "to stabilize greenhouse gas concentrations in the atmosphere at a level that would prevent dangerous anthropogenic

interference with the climate system.... within a time-frame sufficient to allow ecosystems to adapt naturally to climate change, to ensure that food production is not threatened and to enable economic development to proceed in a sustainable manner."[7] Industrialized countries who signed the agreement made an additional, more specific commitment: to aim to stabilize their annual greenhouse gas emissions at 1990 levels by the year 2000.

Five years later, against a backdrop of growing public concern and mounting scientific evidence of the human influence on global climate, the United Nations convened another international conference in Kyoto, Japan. One of the goals of the 1997 Kyoto Conference was to go beyond merely stabilizing greenhouse gas emissions and begin a series of stepped reductions. Scientists estimated that to slow the pace of atmospheric warming, reductions of between 50 and 60 percent ultimately would be necessary. The Kyoto Conference delegates, after days and nights of high-pressure negotiations, agreed to average reductions of 5.2 percent below 1990 levels by the year 2012, a pensive first step towards the larger scale reductions scientists agreed would be necessary. The Kyoto Protocol, as the agreement has come to be known, will not come into force until it has been ratified (approved) by the governments of at least 55 countries, including enough industrialized countries to account for 55 percent of the global carbon dioxide emissions in 1990.

Despite the modest average greenhouse gas reductions it sets forth, the Kyoto Protocol has been fiercely opposed by many nations and multinational corporations whose economies depend heavily on petroleum and coal production. In both Canada and the United States, this opposition has coalesced into a massive lobby campaign aimed at the federal governments in an attempt to forestall so-called carbon taxes and binding regulations on emissions limits. Consequently, the national greenhouse gas reduction plans of both countries are based on weak voluntary measures, and no legislation has been passed by either country to cap or regulate greenhouse gas emissions or to mandate more stringent energy-efficiency standards.

Not surprisingly, North America's emissions of greenhouse gases have continued to rise unabated. By 1998, Canada's emissions were 13 percent higher and in the United States emissions were 11 percent higher than 1990 levels, despite early assurances from industry that voluntary measures would be sufficient for the task. Without major new initiatives to reduce emissions, by 2010 our automobiles, factories and homes could be putting 30 to 35 percent more greenhouse gas into the atmosphere than we agreed to under the Kyoto Protocol.

The Kyoto Protocol is on thin ice. Not only will major industrialized nations such as the United States, Great Britain, and Canada likely fail to reach the greenhouse gas reductions they have committed to under the agreement, but the Protocol itself has yet to be ratified by the governments of any industrialized nations (small island nations and developing nations are

The Framework Convention on Climate Change

THE UNITED NATIONS FRAMEWORK CONVENTION on Climate Change is an agreement among nations to work cooperatively to reduce global greenhouse gas emissions, to encourage sustainable economic development, and to provide assistance to countries that are most vulnerable to the adverse effects of climate change. It places the largest responsibility on industrialized countries because they are the largest emitters of greenhouse gases. In signing the United Nations Framework Convention on Climate Change, developed nations agreed to:

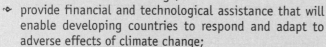

Arthur Feid

- implement national programs to reduce greenhouse gas emissions and protect carbon sinks and reservoirs (e.g., forests, oceans);
- promote research and public education on climate change;
- provide financial and technological assistance that will enable developing countries to respond and adapt to adverse effects of climate change;

One of the most important aspects of the Framework Convention is that it outlines a process through which the international community can agree on actions to be taken and can periodically make amendments (or "protocols") in response to new information about the impact of humans on climate. The Kyoto Protocol of 1997, for instance, called for greater reductions in greenhouse gases than had previously been negotiated.

National representatives who signed The Framework Convention and the Kyoto Protocol signalled their support of these treaties; however, a nation does not become a party to the treaty until it passes a law in its national parliament and sends this "instrument of ratification" (approval) to the United Nations. To ensure that nations who ratify an agreement do not have to act alone, the treaties are not legally binding on any country until they have been ratified by a certain agreed-upon number of nations whose greenhouse gas emissions, together, represent a significant proportion of the global total. The Framework Convention came into force in 1994 and has been ratified by more than 185 countries. The Kyoto Protocol is not yet in force.

— *Gail Littlejohn*

the only ones to do so to date). To further complicate matters, many of the Protocol's signatory nations are locked in fractious debates over such issues as the legitimacy of counting reforestation and soil conservation as carbon sinks, and the responsibility of developing nations in reducing global greenhouse gas emissions.

The world is clearly headed in the wrong direction. Even assuming limited international progress towards reducing greenhouse gas emissions through the Framework Convention on Climate Change, greenhouse gases will continue to accumulate in the atmosphere. This means significant climate change appears to be inevitable. For a northern country such as Canada with its abundant fresh water and natural resources and stable population, climate change may appeal to a short-sighted few as a good thing. But for the majority of people around the world, climate change could be the final destabilizing factor in an already precarious existence. The nations most vulnerable to the effects of climate change are those with dense and rapidly growing populations, particularly in sub-Saharan Africa and in coastal tropical regions. In Bangladesh, a country with a population density of 950 per square kilometer, a one-meter rise in sea level could displace 13 million people.[8] Island nations such as the Maldives could be completely submerged.

Back in 1992, we looked forward to 2000 as the year we would have taken the first step towards gaining control of our greenhouse gas emissions by bringing them down to their 1990 levels. As we look back on our failure to achieve this modest first step, we must question the effectiveness of a purely voluntary approach to reducing greenhouse gas emissions. With every year of inaction on climate change, the cost and difficulty of reducing emissions rises sharply. What is lacking is a willingness on the part of federal, state and provincial governments to implement binding regulations to reduce greenhouse gas emissions.

Our success in remodelling our communities and economy to confront climate change depends partly on how seriously we educators take our role in helping our students become literate and effective global citizens. The curricula in science, social studies, geography, health, and several other subjects are rich with opportunities to introduce students to the issue of climate change. Along with discussion of the science, impacts, and international measures to deal with

climate change, there must be opportunity to learn about the multiple benefits to human health and the environment of climate change solutions such as renewable energy, energy efficiency, and reduced materials consumption.

From a practical perspective, schools are well-placed to make the reduction in greenhouse gas emissions that government and industry seem unwilling to take seriously. Schools consume vast quantities of energy and other resources, and this in itself presents many conservation opportunities. Schools have the additional advantage of being able to combine conservation strategies with education programs that make important links between lifestyle choices and the future of the planet. It is our responsibility as educators to prepare the next generation to respond appropriately to life's future challenges. The threat of global climate change is almost certain to be one of those challenges. ◈

Louise Comeau is the Director of the Sustainable Communities Department of the Federation of Canadian Municipalities in Ottawa, Ontario. Dave Mussell is an Education Program Specialist at the Pembina Institute for Appropriate Development in Drayton Valley, Alberta.

Per Capita Greenhouse Gas Emissions

Per capita emissions are significantly higher in North America and Australia than in European and Asian countries. — *Adapted from a graph by BC Ministry of Environment, Lands and Parks. Data sources: Environment Canada, International Data Bank, Statistics Canada, UNFCCC. Data are for 1996.*

Notes

1   See World Meteorological Organization/United Nations Environmental Programme, Intergovernmental Panel on Climate Change, *Climate Change 2001: The Scientific Basis, Summary for Policymakers*, 2001, pp. 12-16, http://www.ipcc.ch/.

2   NASA Goddard Institute for Space Studies, "Global Temperature Trends: 1998 Global Temperature Smashes Record," December 16, 1998, http://www.giss.nasa.gov/research/observe/surftemp/.

3   R.A. Warrick et al, "Changes in Sea Level" in *Climate Change 1995: The Science of Climate Change*, pp. 359-405.

4   The Intergovernmental Panel on Climate Change was jointly established by the World Meteorological Organization and the United Nations Environment Programme in 1988. Its mandate is to assess scientific information about climate change and associated environmental and socioeconomic impacts, and to formulate response strategies.

5   IPCC, 2001.

6   British Columbia Ministry of Environment, Lands and Parks, "State of Environment Reporting, Greenhouse Gas Indicator," http://www.env.gov.bc.ca/sppl/soerpt/05-4-greenhouse-gas.html, March 30, 2001.

7   Article 2, United Nations Framework Convention on Climate Change, 1992, see http://www.unfccc.org/resource/conv.html.

8   R.J. Nicholls and S.P. Leatherman, "Global Sea-Level Rise," in K.M. Strzpek and J.M. Smith, ed., *As Climate Changes: International Impacts and Implications* (Cambridge University Press, 1995).

Further reading

Understanding Climate Change: A Beginner's Guide to the UN Framework Convention is a very readable discussion for middle and high school students of the potential impacts of climate change and the objectives of the UN Framework Convention on Climate Change. Visit http://www.unfccc.org/resource/beginner.html or contact UNEP/IUC, Geneva Executive Center, Box 356, 1219 Châtelaine, Switzerland.

The Educational Challenges: A Framework for Teaching about Climate Change

by Milton McClaren and William Hammond

T he whole of modern society depends on an act of technological wizardry. Every day we import from the remote past stored solar energy trapped in the form of fossil fuels. This concentrated energy enables us to sustain the current population of humans and to carry on the industrial activities on which the majority of us rely. Every flight of a modern jetliner is the result of burning, in a few hours, solar energy that took thousands, if not hundreds of thousands of years to accumulate through natural processes. But as the old saying goes, there is no such thing as a free lunch. There is growing evidence that the gaseous by-products of our fossil-fuelled technology and lifestyle are enhancing the Earth's natural atmospheric greenhouse effect and changing the climate of our planet.[1]

Climate change is a complex topic, and a good foundation of conceptual knowledge and facts is required before students can reason about it critically and effectively. Moreover, misconceptions abound and are sometimes reinforced by dismally poor media coverage of climate issues and extreme weather events. It is vitally important for curriculum developers and teachers to appreciate the dimensions of climate change as an educational challenge and to approach it responsibly. This statement should not be taken as advocating inaction or avoidance of the topic in school programs, as some would advocate.[2] Quite the opposite. Teaching about climate change is a test of the maturity and sophistication of environmental education. It is a test demanding that teachers and curriculum developers apply the very best approaches to developing students' understanding, reasoning, critical thinking and conceptual finesse.

The following are five fundamental concepts on which any well designed program of climate change education must be based.[3]

1. Change is the norm in Earth's natural systems.

The Earth is constantly changing. Its geological record provides ample evidence that there have been major changes to land forms, climate, and life in the past. There is no reason to expect that the processes which shape the Earth have been suspended. While humans are now implicated in significant global changes, they are not responsible for, or in control of, all global change processes.[4]

2. Earth's systems are linked in complex interactions.

We now have a much more complex picture than we had in the past of the Earth as an interacting, changing, evolving system of systems: an atmobiogeosphere. Processes in the oceans affect the climate; life in forests affects rivers, which in turn affect offshore life on continental shelves and in bays and estuaries. The cycling of minerals and gases is influenced by soil microbes. In short, the Earth is an integrated metasystem in which the connections between elements, while often subtle and even unexpected, can have powerful consequences when broken or damaged.[5]

3. Global changes affect all life.

The fact that Earth is an integrated system means that global changes affect all life, often in unexpected or subtle ways. Even fairly small changes in climate, ocean currents, forest coverage, and the distribution of deserts can sometimes significantly affect the distribution of species. Threatened species can be driven into extinction by loss of habitat; others may invade new territories and compete with natives; parasitic or disease-causing organisms may spread into regions where they were previously unknown or rare.

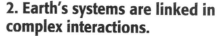

Illustrations by Tom Goldsmith

5

The depletion of ozone in the upper atmosphere can result in increased levels of ground level ultraviolet radiation, causing genetic defects, cancers and other more subtle damage to plant, animal, and microbial species.[6] While humans may be able to take technological or other measures to protect themselves from these changes, other life forms on which we depend for food or resources may not be so fortunate.

4. Local, regional and global changes are often linked.

While the Earth's climate is a global system, humans and other life forms experience it in the form of local weather events. Small changes in the average global temperature may seem insignificant, but they can result in important changes to local weather and conditions affected by weather. Thus, local drought, floods, extreme winter conditions or intense summer heat can all result from changes in the global climate. A single event such as the occurrence of an El Niño or La Niña in the Pacific Ocean can generate widely different impacts around the world. In one area the effect may be increased rainfall; in another, drought; in yet another, hurricanes or tornadoes. It is often hard for people to appreciate that events so different can have a single source, that global changes will play out differently in different regions. Moreover, where human populations are concentrated in large urban areas, many of which are located in coastal plains and river basins, extreme weather events can be catastrophic while the same events taking place where there are few people seem insignificant.[7]

5. Humans have become major agents in global change.

Humans are not the only actors on the global change stage. The Earth has a history that extends far beyond the time period in which our species developed, and global changes, including major climate changes, were occurring continually long before the first appearance of humans. However, the human population has now exceeded six billion, and our use of energy, tools and resources, combined with our numbers, make us a significant factor in current global changes. Human settlement, agriculture, forestry, mining and fishing have all had a profound impact on biodiversity, soil erosion, water quality, and even local and regional climates. Because we are capable of learning, advanced reasoning and communicating, we should be able to modify our behavior when faced with clear indications that we may be on a course for disaster. We should be able to use the tools and resources at our disposal in a more intelligent way so that we can begin to live in harmony with the planet rather than at war with it. Whether we will be able to make the transition to genuine sustainability remains to be seen. This is quite likely the most important challenge facing humankind.[8]

These five concepts are of vital importance for the design and implementation of any program of global change education, whether that program focuses on climate change, loss of biodiversity, population growth, or patterns of resource exploitation and agriculture. Modern research in cognitive science clearly demonstrates the importance of conceptual schemata for learning. Without such frameworks for thinking and organizing information, students and teachers alike are often overwhelmed by a mass of information and the curriculum becomes nothing more than a content scramble.

It is therefore of vital importance for educational materials to present the Earth as it is: a vital, changing, evolving planet. It is essential for the human story to be set in a geological perspective so that students appreciate what a short tenure modern humans have had on Earth. It is also important to invite students to appreciate how human activities may influence natural systems, as in enhancing the natural greenhouse effect. But it is equally important for students to appreciate that some of the changes that are occurring and that will occur on Earth are neither caused by our actions nor subject to our intervention. The problem of earthquake prediction is a good example. Human activities seem to have little if anything to do with the geophysical processes that generate earth movements. While our entire view of seismic activity has been transformed in the last 60 years or so by the development of the concept of plate tectonics,[9] we still have grave difficulty predicting when earthquakes will occur, although we can definitely identify regions where they are highly probable. While we can take wise precautions against the impact of quakes on our buildings and other constructions, and prepare ourselves to deal with major quakes when they occur, we can do nothing to stop them.

When students are presented with facts about massive, long term, global forces and change processes there is a danger that they may adopt attitudes of indifference or resignation. After all, if humans are so insignificant why should we bother trying to do anything at all to moderate our fairly trivial impact on the Earth? This calls for educational approaches in which risk factors and long term costs and benefits as well as ideas such as the precautionary principle become subjects for debate and critical inquiry. Students also need to learn how different disciplines approach the subject of global change. While science can reveal the nature and causes of global changes, science does not automatically determine what actions we should take in the light of this knowledge. Many decisions about human impacts on global climate, for example, are political and economic in nature and these forms of knowledge are different from science or mathematics. For educators, the complexity of global climate change is both a problem and an asset. Because the topic is multidisciplinary, it is an ideal vehicle for the development of students' conceptual finesse: their ability to appreciate and apply different forms of knowledge and reasoning and to recognize how these forms differ. However, the complex and multidisciplinary nature of global change as a topic demands sophisticated teaching strategies and collaboration among teachers in different subject fields.

6

Critics of global climate education sometimes argue that it should be approached scientifically and that only scientific facts that are known without any uncertainty should be taken into consideration.[10] This view would eviscerate the topic of climate change of its educational potential and present students with a very impoverished understanding of it. However, as many teachers fully appreciate, it is difficult for a science teacher discussing the chemistry of ozone depletion by chlorofluorocarbons (CFCs) to address students' questions concerning the economic problems of removing CFCs from appliances in developing countries. The best way to deal with this question is therefore to let students hear from other specialists, either directly or vicariously through books, articles, the Internet, and visiting speakers, and through interdisciplinary instructional approaches that employ effective team teaching.

The issue of scientific certainty is also an important and inescapable element of effective education about global climate change. It is very important for students not only to understand what is known about climate change but also to appreciate how this knowledge has developed, and how reliable it is. It is an essential attribute of effective science education, and, for that matter, of any education, that students be invited into communities of practice or scholarship. They should be allowed to witness the difficulties and uncertainties of research as well as its triumphs and firm conclusions. They should be let in on the arguments and debates that make research and inquiry so lively and engaging. They should be presented with information in ways that invite them to consider how current, how reliable, and how widely accepted it is. This does not weaken the educational power of environmental education; it strengthens it.

This is not, however, to argue that all opinions and points of view should be presented as having equal validity and currency in the community of scholars, as some who advocate "balanced" presentation of all environmental problems and issues would have us believe. The president of the Flat Earth Society is not given equal time in every news report about the flight of a space shuttle.[11] Nor should the fact that most science is tentative and ongoing in nature be used as an argument to defer all action until absolute certainty develops. Here again, the educational power of discussing climate change research can be developed only if students evaluate and debate the bases on which proposals for action are made, considering costs and benefits and the risks of both action and inaction. Where scientific uncertainty exists, students should be encouraged to understand why it exists: is the problem with fundamental theory, with insufficient data, with poorly developed data

gathering instruments, or with lack of funding for basic research? Where political arguments exist concerning which measures should be taken to address human effects on climate, students should be invited to ask whether the differences arise because the advocates of different positions are using different scientific facts, reasoning from different economic models, using different studies of public support and attitudes, or starting from different ideological premises.

The most inadequate possible educational response to uncertainty and argument is to ignore them, or to present only that which is not contentious. Once again, it is essential for students to appreciate the differences between scientific, economic, political, religious, philosophical or other forms of argument. This is especially important given the tendency of modern mass media and political discourse to blur these distinctions. We should also pose a variety of alternatives for students to consider. These might include:

Students need to learn how different disciplines approach the subject of global change. While scientists can reveal the nature and causes of global changes, science does not automatically determine what actions we should take in the light of this knowledge.

↝ assuming that our activities are having no serious impacts and simply letting what will happen, happen;

↝ assuming that humans are key contributors to current global changes and that we should take action to reduce our impacts or to eliminate those which are damaging to the biogeosphere;

↝ assuming that we do not have enough scientific evidence of global change and that we should wait until we have definitive scientific evidence before taking any substantial action to reduce human impacts, especially if action is likely to have serious economic implications.

Students could then develop scenarios for the mid-range future based on the different assumptions and defend or propose various courses of action within the context of their chosen positions.

Any effective educational program addressing global climate change must confront the fact that many, many students have serious deficiencies in their basic conceptions and knowledge of earth science as well as chemistry, physics and biology. Studies of scientific misconceptions among college graduates, for example, show that even science majors in some of the finest universities often harbor importantly flawed ideas about basic processes such as the seasons, the process of photosynthesis and its relation to biogeophysical cycles, the composition of the atmosphere, and the role of solar energy in the operation of the Earth's major systems.[12] What these findings imply is that it is of great importance to assess students' prior knowledge before proceeding with programs of instruction. Research on cognitive schemata and learning affirms the power that misconceptions exert on reasoning. That research also indicates that if learning is a constructive activity, it also sometimes requires the deconstruction or unlearning of existing cognitive structures. This usually requires far more time and attention than is given to it in school programs.

A useful approach is to develop some simple tests of prior knowledge which can be given to students at the opening of a program of instruction. The tests can assess basic factual knowledge through questions asking about the relative percentages of gases in the atmosphere or the source of weight gain in plants as they grow from seed to maturity. Some of these questions can take the form of simple multiple choice, true or false, or matching items. However, it is also useful and revealing to ask students to make drawings, diagrams and graphs, or to engage in narrative discussions about various processes. It is also important to find out why students get answers wrong on these tests, to probe below the surface of presented responses in order to appreciate the reasoning behind them.

For prior knowledge assessment to be effective, students must work in an atmosphere of intellectual safety. The point of prior knowledge assessment is not to classify or rank students, but to gain an appreciation of the range of concepts in a class and the status of students' basic knowledge in order to plan more effective instruction. While prior knowledge assessment often focuses on basic scientific knowledge and concepts, it can also address forms of reasoning, values and attitudes. For example, the work of Kempton, Boster and Hartley (1996) on environmental values and American culture revealed that many people reasoned about greenhouse gas emissions using knowledge and understanding of CFC ozone depletion. In other words, they reasoned that if the problem of CFCs had been "fixed" by the simple technical expedient of replacing CFCs as propellants, refrigerants and cleaning agents, the same could be done for carbon dioxide.[13] If teachers or curriculum designers are aware of this sort of reasoning, their designs for instruction and learning experiences can take these prior conceptual structures into account. Of course, assessments of both program effectiveness and student learning should return to review the same basic knowledge, concepts and reasoning processes.

To conclude, there is good news and bad news about education that addresses global climate change. The bad news is that the topic is complex and challenging. The good news is also that it is complex and challenging. We are sure that there are many teachers and program developers who are willing to accept the challenge and that there are researchers and other educators prepared to help them. §

Milton McClaren is an Emeritus Professor of Education in the Faculty of Education at Simon Fraser University in Burnaby, British Columbia. William Hammond is an Assistant Professor in the College of Arts and Sciences and Faculty of Education at Florida Gulf Coast University in Fort Myers, Florida.

Notes

1 Citing increases in global average surface temperature of 0.15 ± 0.05°C per decade since 1979, the Intergovernmental Panel on Climate Change concluded in 2001 that most of the warming observed over the last 50 years is due to the increase in greenhouse gas concentrations attributable to human activities. See *Climate Change 2001: The Scientific Basis, Summary for Policymakers*, the World Meteorological Organization/United Nations Environmental Programme, Intergovernmental Panel on Climate Change, 2001, http://www.ipcc.ch/.

2 M. Sanera and J.S. Shaw, *Facts not Fear: A Parent's Guide to Teaching Children About the Environment* (Washington, DC: Regnery, 1996).

3 These five foundational concepts resulted from discussions among some of the leading scientists currently working to understand the human dimensions of global change, including climate change, during a decade of summer seminars, beginning in 1990, sponsored by the Aspen Global Change Institute (AGCI) in Aspen, Colorado. These sessions were attended by researchers from academic institutions, government agencies, private bodies, and corporations around the world. Their discussions covered the physical, chemical, biological, geological, economic, demographic, sociocultural and political dimensions of global change. In addition to these sessions, AGCI, with support from NASA, has since 1997 offered summer education programs for teachers in Canada and the U.S. These short courses bring educators together with leading climate change scientists to develop better understanding of climate change and to discuss the educational challenges presented by the topic. Both the AGCI summer science seminars and the teacher short courses have added greatly to our appreciation of the educational dimensions of global change and have created a network of connections between educators and researchers working in the field.

4 S.H. Schneider and R. Londer, *The Coevolution of Climate and Life* (San Francisco: Sierra Club Books, 1994); S.H. Schneider, *Laboratory Earth: The Planetary Gamble We Can't Afford to Lose* (New York: Basic Books, 1997).

5 "Managing Planet Earth," *Scientific American* (special issue, September, 1989).

6 S. Cagin and. P. Dray. *Between Earth and Sky: How CFCs Changed Our World and Endangered the Ozone Layer* (New York: Pantheon, 1993).

7 R.P. Turco, *Earth Under Siege: Air Pollution and Global Change* (New York: Oxford University Press, 1995).

8 J.T. Houghton, B.A. Callander and S.K. Varney, eds., *Climate Change: The IPCC Scientific Assessment*. Report by the World Meteorological Organization/United Nations Environment Program, Intergovernmental Panel on Climate Change (New York: Cambridge University Press, 1990); Turco, 1995.

9 T.J. Crowley and G.R. North, *Paleoclimatology* (New York: Oxford University Press, 1991).

10 Sanera and Shaw, 1996.

11 S.H. Schneider, personal communication, August 1998.

12 *Eliciting Student Ideas*, video produced by Harvard Smithsonian Center for Astrophysics (Boston, MA: The Private Universe Project, The Annenburg/CPB Math Science Project, 1995).

13 W. Kempton, J.S. Boster and J.A. Hartley, *Environmental Values in American Culture* (Cambridge, MA: Massachusetts Institute of Technology Press, 1996).

Other references

Aspen Global Change Institute. *Ground Truth Studies Teacher Handbook*. British Columbia ed. Victoria, BC: British Columbia Ministry of Environment, Lands, and Parks, 1994.

Bransford, J.D., A.L. Brown, and R.R. Cocking, eds. *How People Learn: Brain, Mind, Experience, and School*. Committee on Developments in the Science of Learning, Commission on Behavioral and Social Sciences and Education, National Research Council. Washington, DC: National Academy Press, 1999.

Calvin, W.H. "The Great Climate Flip-flop." *Atlantic Monthly* (January 1998): 47-64.

Fulkerson, W., R.R. Judkins, and M.J. Sanghvi. "Energy from Fossil Fuels." *Scientific American* 263 (September 1990): 128-135.

FY [fiscal year] 2000 U.S. Global Change Research Program. Subcommittee on Global Change Research, Committee on Environment and Natural Resources of the National Science and Technology Council. *Our Changing Planet*. Washington, DC: Office of Science and Technology Planning, 1999.

Holdren, J.P. "Energy in Transition." *Scientific American* 263 (September 1990): 156-163.

Lovins, A. *World Energy Strategies: Facts, Issues, and Options*. New York: Harper Colophon, 1980.

"Reading the Patterns." *The Economist* (April 1-7, 1995): 65-67.

Somerville, R.C.J. *The Forgiving Air: Understanding Environmental Change*. Berkeley: The University of California Press, 1996.

The Greenhouse Effect

by Louise Comeau and Tim Grant

About half of the radiant energy that comes from the sun is reflected back into space after striking reflective surfaces such as particles in the atmosphere or snow at ground level. The rest is absorbed at the Earth's surface and released as infrared, or heat, energy. As this heat radiates upwards, some escapes into space and some is absorbed and emitted back to Earth by gases, such as water vapor, carbon dioxide, nitrous oxide and methane, which occur naturally in the atmosphere. This natural "greenhouse" effect is what makes the Earth's surface warm enough to support life. Without greenhouse gases, the average temperature on Earth would be about -18°C (0.4°F).

As long as the energy entering the system is balanced by the energy leaving, average temperatures remain relatively stable. But a rise in levels of greenhouse gases has the potential to upset this equilibrium by increasing the amount of heat that gets trapped near the Earth's surface. For most of the last 10,000 years, the concentration of the most abundant greenhouse gas, carbon dioxide, remained fairly steady at 280 parts per million (280 molecules of carbon dioxide for every million molecules of air). During that period, there existed a balance between sources of carbon dioxide such as respiration, decomposition and forest fires, and processes that remove it from the atmosphere such as photosynthesis and absorption by oceans.

Since the Industrial Revolution began in the 1750s, humans have affected the carbon dioxide balance in two ways. We have added large quantities of carbon dioxide to the atmosphere by burning carbon-rich fossil fuels such as coal, oil and natural gas. At the same time, we have cut down nearly half of the world's forests,[1] releasing the carbon stored in the trees and reducing the

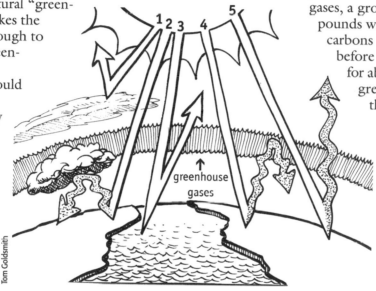

Tom Goldsmith

Pathways of solar radiation:

1. Light strikes particles in the atmosphere and is reflected back to space.
2. Light is absorbed at the surface and released as heat; then absorbed by clouds and emitted back to Earth.
3. Light strikes water and is reflected back to space.
4. Light is absorbed at the surface and released as heat; then absorbed by greenhouse gases and emitted back to Earth.
5. Light is absorbed at the surface and released as heat; the heat escapes directly into space.

Earth's ability to absorb carbon dioxide through photosynthesis. In the past decade, almost seven billion tonnes of carbon were released every year by the burning of fossil fuels and destruction of forests. About half of it dissolved in the oceans or was taken up by plants; the other half, about 3.5 billion tonnes of carbon, was added to the atmosphere and will remain there for 50 to 200 years. So far, the global concentration of CO_2 has increased by 31% from pre-industrial levels and is estimated to be increasing at the rate of 0.4% per year. Methane levels have increased by 151% and nitrous oxide by 17%. The most potent of greenhouse gases, a group of human-made compounds which includes chlorofluorocarbons (CFCs), did not even exist before the 1930s, but they account for about 12% of today's enhanced greenhouse effect.[2] All of these greenhouse gases are destroyed over time by atmospheric chemistry, but the process can take decades to centuries.

What can we expect?

Adding more greenhouse gases to the atmosphere than can be disposed of naturally is like adding an extra blanket to your bed: things are going to heat up. According to climate scientists, mean surface temperatures will likely rise between 1.4 and 5.8°C by 2100.[3] Warming will not be the same the world over. Because of the way wind and ocean currents transfer energy from the equator to the poles, and as snow and ice melt, the region north of 50° N is expected to warm more than the global average. Summer temperatures could increase by as much as 7°C in Canada's Mackenzie Basin, with increases of up to 9°C in April and May.[4]

Because heat is what drives the climate system, we can expect an increase in extreme weather. Among the many impacts of climate change that scientists now predict are: a rise in sea level and changes in currents; changes in precipitation patterns; shifts of temperature zones; an increase in the frequency and intensity of storms; more heat waves and droughts; and a higher incidence of forest fires.

We are already seeing these effects in North America. Karl et al reported in the February 1996 *Bulletin of the American Meteorological Society* that there is less than a one in 1,000 chance that the observed increase in extreme one-day precipitation events in the United States could be a naturally occurring event. In the north, the Mackenzie Basin has warmed by an average of 1.5°C over the last 100 years,[5] more than double the global rate (0.6°C). Alaska and eastern Siberia have warmed at similar rates.

What can be done?

To slow the pace of climate change, we will have to reduce overall greenhouse gas emissions from many sources, but especially carbon emissions associated with fossil fuel consumption and the clearing of tropical rainforests. In North America, most analysts agree that we need to eliminate subsidies to the oil, gas and coal industries while promoting energy efficiency, renewable energy technologies, and the development of transportation systems that allow people to leave their cars at home. Many argue for "carbon taxes" on the use of fossil fuels that would encourage more resource-efficient activities. Much research has shown that taking steps to reduce carbon emissions actually enhances economic development. In a 1996 study, the Sierra Club of Canada found that stabilizing and reducing greenhouse

gas emissions in Canada could create up to 1.5 million person-years of work, far in excess of the job creation potential of the current oil sands expansion in northern Alberta.

To reduce carbon dioxide emissions in the short term, the single most effective measure, and the least disruptive economically, would be to raise the fuel efficiency standards of new cars and trucks which have remained unchanged for almost a decade. On an individual level, planting trees, favoring public transit and bicycles over cars, making our homes more energy-efficient, reusing and recycling materials, and eating locally-grown foods are actions that everyone can take to help reduce emissions of greenhouse gases. ◊

Louise Comeau is the Director of the Sustainable Communities Department of the Federation of Canadian Municipalities in Ottawa, Ontario. Tim Grant ("What Can Be Done?") is co-editor of Green Teacher *magazine.*

Notes

[1] Lester R. Brown, et al., *State of the World 1999* (Washington, DC: Worldwatch Institute, 1999), p. 60.

[2] Intergovernmental Panel on Climate Change (IPPC), *Climate Change 2001: The Scientific Basis, Summary for Policymakers*, World Meteorological Organization/ United Nations Environmental Programme, p. 7.

[3] IPCC, p. 13.

[4] Janet Brotton and Geoffrey Wall, "The Possible Effect of Climate Change on the Sport Hunting of Bathurst Caribou of the NWT," Mackenzie Basin Impact Study, Interim Report #2, 1994.

[5] Environment Canada, *The State of Canada's Climate: Monitoring Variability and Change*, 1995.

The Major Greenhouse Gases

Gas	Contribution to the greenhouse effect	Increase since 1750	Heat-trapping ability (in relation to CO_2)	Lifespan in atmosphere (years)	Sources
Carbon dioxide (CO_2)	53%	31%	1	50-200	Respiration; decomposition; forest fires; evaporation from oceans; burning of fossil fuels.
Methane (CH_4)	17%	151%	25	10	Underground deposits (natural gas is mostly methane); respiration by anaerobic decomposers living in wetlands, rice paddies and the digestive tracts of ruminant animals and termites; garbage dumps.
Nitrous oxide (N_2O)	5%	17%	200	150	Microbes that break down organic matter in soils; nitrogen fertilizers; burning of fossil fuels and wood.
Ground-level ozone (O_3)	13%	36%	2,000	weeks	Very small amounts naturally present in atmosphere; formed photochemically when nitrogen oxides and volatile organic compounds in automobile exhaust react in sunlight.
Halocarbons (CFCs)	12%	none in 1750	up to 10,000	60-100	Human-made compounds used in refrigerators, air conditioners, foam products, aerosol sprays. There are no natural sources.

Gases and Greenhouses: Simple Activities for Exploring Key Concepts

by Gail Littlejohn and Alex Waters

Gases Have No Borders

Concept: Diffusion is the movement of gas molecules from places of high concentration to places of lower concentration. Greenhouse gases diffuse outward from their sources and become mixed in the atmosphere.

Method: Put a small amount of a strong smelling (and non-allergenic) substance such as vinegar or peppermint oil onto a cloth or kleenex. Stand on one side of the classroom and wave the cloth. Ask students to raise their hands as soon as they detect the odor, and time how long it takes for everyone to smell it. Discuss the role of diffusion (and wind) in making greenhouse gas emissions a global problem.

Gases Like Water

Concepts: An important property of gases is that they dissolve in water. Dissolved oxygen is essential for the underwater respiration of aquatic organisms, and the ability of carbon dioxide to dissolve in liquid is what enables us to enjoy cold, fizzy beverages on hot summer days. Carbon dioxide is about 200 times more water-soluble than oxygen, and this high solubility means that it easily moves between the atmosphere and bodies of water on the Earth's surface. The world's oceans are referred to as carbon "sinks" and "reservoirs" because they take up huge quantities of CO_2, either directly or through photosynthesis carried out by surface phytoplankton which later decompose on the ocean floor. (Carbon dioxide is also taken up by land plants through photosynthesis, but it is returned to the atmosphere when plants decompose or are destroyed by fire.) About half of the CO_2 emitted by the burning of fossil fuels in the past few decades has been taken up by oceans and forests.

Purpose: To demonstrate that there is oxygen dissolved in tap water and that it dissolves more readily in cold water than in warm.

Method:

1. Put equal amounts of cold aerated tap water into two beakers.

2. Place one beaker on a hot plate or over a bunsen burner at low heat.

3. Observe the bubbles forming on the bottoms and sides of the beakers and make comparisons between the warm and cold water. The warmer the water is, the less air that will remain dissolved in it. As a result, air bubbles will form more quickly (come out of solution) in the heated sample.

Gases Are Weighty

Purpose: To demonstrate that CO_2 has weight and to show the effect of temperature and pressure on the solubility of CO_2 (see Concepts discussion in the previous activity).

Method:

1. Prepare a warm-water bath by heating 100 ml of water to 50°C (120°F) in a 500 ml beaker.

2. Using an electronic balance, find and record the masses of two unopened cans of chilled, carbonated pop (dry off any condensate on the outside of each can before weighing).

3. Carefully open both cans, retaining the metal tabs. Discuss what causes the characteristic "whoosh" sound. *(An increase in pressure increases the solubility of any gas in water. Carbonated drinks are bottled under pressure; when the can is opened, the pressure in the can drops until it is in equilibrium with the atmosphere. As pressure drops, carbon dioxide begins to come out of the liquid.)*

4. Wait three minutes to allow some of the gas to escape from the cans. Measure and record the temperature of each liquid while waiting.

5. Place one of the cans in the warm-water bath. After 10-12 minutes, remove the heated can from the water and dry off the outsides of both cans.

6. Measure and record the temperature of each liquid and the mass of each can. Compare the mass before and after to determine the weight of the CO_2 that has escaped from each can.

Based on your observations, are some areas of the world's oceans likely to hold more carbon than others? *(Of the Earth's estimated 42 trillion tons of carbon, about 1 trillion tons are in the surface water of oceans and 38 trillion tons are in the ocean depths where temperature is lower and pressure is greater. The transfer of CO_2 from atmosphere to ocean — the "sink" — occurs most readily in regions where surface waters are colder; warm equatorial surface waters are often sources of rather than sinks for atmospheric CO_2).*

Greenhouse Gas Pursuit

Purpose: To become familiar with characteristics and sources of the major greenhouse gases.

Method: Divide the class into groups of three or four and ask each group to generate six of more questions related to one of the major greenhouse gases (excluding water vapor). They are: carbon dioxide, methane, nitrous oxide, ground-level ozone and CFCs (see chart on page 10). A sixth group could be assigned the topic of the greenhouse effect. Examples of questions: "You might find me rising from a rice paddy" (*methane*); "I can hang around in the atmosphere for up to 200 years" (*carbon dioxide*). Put questions and answers on sheets of paper divided into a six-block grid. Photocopy the sheets and cut them into sets of question cards. Have teams challenge each other (making sure that teams are not asked their own questions!).

Mayonnaise Jar Greenhouse

Purpose: To demonstrate the concept of the Earth as a greenhouse.

Materials: 1 large mayonnaise jar with lid; 2 small thermometers; 2 pieces of cardboard; rubber bands; bright desk lamp or sunny window

Introduction for students
A greenhouse is a building especially constructed for growing plants when the weather outside is cold. The walls of a greenhouse are made of glass or clear plastic. Sunlight passes through the walls, is absorbed by the soil and plants, and is then emitted as heat energy which warms the air inside the greenhouse. The walls prevent the heated air from escaping, so it remains trapped inside the greenhouse.

Certain gases in the atmosphere are called greenhouse gases because they act like the glass in a greenhouse. Greenhouse gases allow sunlight to pass house. Greenhouse gases allow sunlight to pass through to the Earth's surface. When sunlight hits the Earth, it heats the surface (think of a blacktop parking lot in the summer). As the heat rises, some of it is trapped by the greenhouse gases. Without the greenhouse gases creating what is called the natural greenhouse effect, the atmosphere and climate on Earth would be too cold to sustain life.

Method:
1. Using rubber bands, attach the top of each thermometer to a piece of cardboard. Make sure the numbers are facing out when you stand the thermometers.

2. Place one of the thermometers inside the jar and put the lid on the jar.

3. Place the jar in a sunny window or beside a desk lamp. Next to it place the second thermometer. Be sure that both thermometers are shaded from direct light by the cardboard (see diagram below).

4. Record the temperatures of both thermometers every 10 minutes for one hour.

5. You might want to continue the experiment and record the two temperatures every day at the same time for a week. Graph the data and discuss how the temperature fluctuates from day to day.

Discussion
↝ Why does the thermometer inside the jar show a higher temperature? *(The glass and lid trap the heated air, so the temperature rises and stays higher than the temperature outside.)*

↝ Would the mayonnaise jar greenhouse be more effective on some days than others, or at certain times of the day? *(Variations will result from different light conditions and the length of exposure to direct sunlight.)*

↝ How is the jar behaving like the Earth's atmosphere? How is it different? *(Like greenhouse gases, the jar traps heat. However, the Earth's atmosphere is not a solid barrier which stops hot air from leaving, as a glass jar does. Some of the heat radiating from the Earth's surface escapes directly into space. Some is absorbed temporarily by greenhouse gases and then emitted back to the Earth's surface.)*

Carbon Dioxide and the Greenhouse Effect

Purpose: To determine the effect of increased levels of carbon dioxide in the atmosphere.

Materials: Two plastic 2-liter pop bottles; ruler; two thermometers (bitherm thermometers are easiest to read); one 150-watt spotlight; light stand; two full, liter-sized bottles of cola or other dark-colored carbonated beverage.

Method:

1. Open one of the soft drinks the day before the experiment. Leave it open overnight or until the carbon dioxide has dissipated and the cola has gone "flat." Do not open the second bottle of cola until just before the experiment begins. Both the flat and the fizzy colas should be at room temperature.

2. Cut off the tops of the empty two-liter bottles to make two open-mouthed bottles 20 cm (8") in height.

3. With a ruler, mark a fill line on the side of each bottle about 8 cm (3.5") up from the bottom. Punch a small hole in the side of each bottle at least 5 cm (2") above the fill line.

4. Fill one bottle to the line with the flat cola. Fill the other bottle with fresh, fizzy cola. DO NOT insert the thermometers until a few minutes before the experiment begins (see step 6), as the bubbles from the freshly-opened pop may splatter the thermometer and subsequently lower the temperature through evaporation.

5. Let the containers stand for 30 to 60 minutes. This allows time for the CO_2 to leave the liquid and slowly fill the air space in the bottle (CO_2 is heavier than air, so it will stay in the container). Students can test whether there is sufficient CO_2 by lowering a match or splint into the bottle. If it goes out, there is enough CO_2.

6. Put the thermometers through the holes in the bottles so their ends are in the middle of the air space above the liquid.

7. Place the bottles at equal distances from the spotlight, approximately 25 cm (10"), and record the temperature in each bottle.

8. Turn on the light. Observe and record the temperature in each bottle every minute for 10 minutes. (Do not let the experiment exceed 10 minutes, as the CO_2 will have dissipated after this time).

Once the experiment begins and the CO_2 warms up, the gas will become lighter and leave the container. However, before this happens, students should notice a temperature increase of as much as 5°C in the CO_2-rich atmosphere.

Alternative set-up: If you have a pressurized soda dispenser with a hose, a quicker method of creating a CO_2-rich atmosphere is to use canisters of CO_2 available from beer supply stores. Instead of cola, place 5 cm (2") of dark, dry soil in the bottoms of the bottles. Discharge one CO_2 canister into the soda dispenser. Then place the soda dispenser hose 2.5 cm (1") from the soil in one bottle and slowly release the CO_2. Repeat, adding a second canister of CO_2 to the same bottle. Record the temperatures, turn on the light, and run the experiment for 10 minutes. ✎

Gail Littlejohn is co-editor of Green Teacher *magazine in Toronto, Ontario. Alex Waters ("Carbon Dioxide and the Greenhouse Effect") is Project Manager for the Centre for Sustainability at the Kortright Centre in Woodbridge, Ontario.*

Credits: *"Mayonnaise Jar Greenhouse" is based on an activity in* Global Warming: Understanding the Forecast, Teachers' Resource Manual *by C.M. Raab and J.E.S. Sokolow (New York, NY: American Museum of Natural History and Environmental Defense Fund, 1992). "Gases Are Weighty" is based on an activity in* Rivers Curriculum Guide: Chemistry *by V. Bryan, A. Burbank and J. Ballinger (Palo Alto: Dale Seymour Publications, 1997).*

References

Brown, Lester R., Christopher Flavin, Hilary French. *State of the World 2001: Worldwatch Institute Report* (New York: Norton, 2001).

Kellogg, William W. "Overview of Global Environmental Change: The Science and Social Science Issues." *Marine Technology Society Journal* 25:3, pp. 5-11.

Takahashi, Taro, Pieter Tans, and Inez Fung. "Balancing the Budget." *Oceanus* 35: 1 (Spring 1992), pp. 18-28.

Understanding Climate Variability

by Gail Littlejohn

When we talk about climate change as a current event, we sometimes forget that the planetary systems that govern climate are never static. Forty-five million years ago, the high Arctic was balmy enough to support redwoods and cedars up to 30 meters tall and a meter in diameter. Eighteen thousand years ago, most parts of Canada and the northern United States were under ice. And nearly everywhere in North America there has been a period since the retreat of the glaciers when the climate was warmer than it is today. In fact, climate change appears to be the rule, not the exception. The difference now, of course, is that it is *our* climate and it is human activities that appear to be setting these changes in motion.

In attempting to determine how much influence humans are having and to predict what the consequences might be, climatologists frequently pose questions about past conditions. For example, a useful question might be: When the level of carbon dioxide in the atmosphere was this high in the past, how warm was the Earth? or How high were sea levels during those times in the past when the Earth was as warm as we think it will be in the future? Knowing about the past can help us understand what is occurring at present and foresee (and perhaps better prepare for) what might happen in the future. For students attempting to grasp the currently unfolding science of climate change, it is additionally helpful to know how scientists acquire and interpret the information we have about the Earth's past.

Gail Littlejohn

Paleobotanists extract a sediment core from Wagner Lake near Uxbridge, Ontario. Fossil pollen preserved in the layers of this lake-bottom mud will give evidence of changes in plant communities and climatic conditions since the retreat of the glaciers.

How do we know about past climate?

If all we had to rely on were thermometer readings, our knowledge of the Earth's climate would reach back only to about 1860 when meteorologists and mariners began taking systematic measurements of temperatures around the world. Fortunately, temperature records are not the only fingerprints of past climate. All living organisms depend to some degree on a certain range of climatic conditions and much has been learned about the past by looking at evidence they have left behind. Three important sources of information are sediment cores, tree rings and glacial ice cores.

Sediment cores

The muddy sediments at the bottoms of oceans and lakes contain particles of soil and ash and the fossil remains of aquatic creatures and plant material that have been deposited layer-upon-layer over eons. By driving hollow tubes into these sediments, scientists extract cores, or long cylinders of mud that can be read like timelines. Each layer provides clues to the local climate at the time the sediments were deposited. For example, fossil pollen in 5,000-year-old lake sediments is evidence of the types and abundance of the plants that lived nearby, and by looking at the modern ranges and communities of these plants we can infer what the climate was like at that time. Other clues are found by analyzing the type, or isotope, of oxygen contained in the calcium carbonate ($CaCO_3$) shells of marine organisms buried in ocean sediments. During periods of glaciation when a higher proportion of annual precipitation stayed frozen on land instead of cycling back to the sea, a lighter isotope of oxygen (oxygen-16) accumulated in ice sheets. Meanwhile, sea water became enriched with a heavier oxygen (oxygen-18), as did the oxygen-containing shells of the sea creatures who lived at that time.

Tree rings

The oldest living trees on Earth are the gnarled bristlecone pines (*Pinus longaeva*) that grow in the White Mountains of eastern California, one of which is estimated to be up to 4,900 years old. By counting and measuring the width of the tree rings, scientists called dendrochronologists track changes in annual growth over thousands of years. They can then correlate these changes with the environmental conditions that likely gave rise to them.

Activity

Have students examine crosscuts ("tree cookies") to determine the age of a tree when it was cut and to look for variations in the width of the rings. Wider rings indicate a year in which climatic conditions were optimal for that species. If you know when and where the tree was cut, try to correlate ring-width patterns with meteorological data on annual temperatures and rainfall during the lifetime of the tree.

Glacier ice

Ice cores extracted from glaciers in Greenland and Antarctica have provided information about past climate change as well as about past concentrations of atmospheric gases. By analyzing the proportions of different isotopes of oxygen and hydrogen at each level of the ice, scientists can determine what the temperature was when the ice was formed; and by analyzing bubbles of "fossil air" trapped in the ice, they can measure the concentration of atmospheric carbon dioxide at that time. Other useful information is gleaned from impurities in the ice: layers of ash and dust, for example, may reflect volcanic activity and high winds.

What causes climate change?

Much is still to be learned about the complex interplay of biogeophysical forces that lead to major shifts in

Gail Littlejohn

Rick Searle

Left: Bristlecone pine in southern California: The annual rings of these oldest living trees tell the story of temperature and precipitation patterns over thousands of years. Right: The uplift of mountain ranges can alter climate by affecting patterns of wind and precipitation.

climate. The following are some of the likely prime movers in these long-term processes.

Earth's position

The position of the Earth in relation to the sun determines the distribution of solar radiation around the globe through the seasons. In 1941, a Serbian scientist named Milankovitch looked beyond these well-known seasonal variations and hypothesized that there are three very long-term cyclic changes in Earth's position which have a major influence on climate. The first Milankovitch cycle is a change in the shape of the Earth's orbit which every 100,000 years takes the Earth further away from the sun at the perihelion (the closest point of the year), resulting in a colder climate. The second cycle, of about 41,000 years' duration, is a shift in the tilt of the Earth's axis from 22° to 25° (currently it is midway at 23.5°). When tilt is greater, polar regions receive more solar radiation in summer and less in winter, a situation that could result in more extreme seasonal temperature variations. Finally, there is a 21,000-year cycle which, every 58 years, advances the perihelion by one day. Presently, the Earth is closest to the sun on January 4, but 10,500 years ago it was closest on about July 4. Northern winters would likely have been colder, but summers would have been hotter. This more intense summer heat is thought to be a likely cause of the melting of the great ice sheets in North America

Activity

Have students create mini-globes by drawing the hemispheres, continents, meridians and latitudes on foam balls. Insert a pencil into the south pole of each ball as a rotational axis. Rotate the globes around a bright lightbulb in a dark room to see how changes in orbital shape (from elliptical to nearly circular), axial tilt (from 22° to 25°), and date of the perihelion (the day when Earth is closest to the sun) might affect the amount of light that strikes different regions.

Tectonic movement

The Earth's tectonic plates are always on the move, although most of us are aware of it only when an earthquake strikes. Yet if we look at the shape of the world's continents, it is easy to imagine them as pieces of a giant jigsaw puzzle which have broken away from each other and drifted apart. This is exactly what is thought to have occurred about 200 million years ago when a large supercontinent called Pangaea ("all earth") split apart. The subsequent rearrangement of land masses may have altered climate by re-routing ocean currents which distribute heat around the globe. Similarly, the uplifting of mountain ranges on land changes temperature and precipitation patterns by altering wind movement.

Activity

Cut out the shapes of the continents and move them around to see how they once fit together in the supercontinent Pangaea. Discuss why the present-day arrangement of the continents might hinder the distribution of heat from the equatorial zone.

Changes in ice and snow cover

Extensive snow and ice cover has a cooling effect, not just because snow is cold but because it reflects rather than absorbs the sun's energy. Cooling leads, in turn, to the accumulation of more ice and snow, which causes even more of the sun's energy to be reflected, which in turn leads to more cooling. This is called a positive feedback effect, and over time it can accelerate climate change. A similar positive feedback loop occurs during warming trends: as ice and snow melt, more radiation is absorbed and released as heat by newly exposed soil surfaces. This heat in turn leads to more melting.

Demonstration

Chill several small paving stones of equal size, color and composition in a refrigerator. Take them out, wrap one in aluminum foil and the others in paper or cloth of various colors, including white and black. Leave one stone uncovered. Place the stones in a sunny window for about 30 minutes; then unwrap them and pass them around. (The stones should hold their temperature long enough for everyone to touch them.) Relate the results to experiences such as feeling the warmth absorbed by a dark jacket on a cold sunny day,

or noticing places where snow melts quickly, such as around a tree trunk or a leaf in a snowbank. If, as scientists believe, average temperatures in the far north are rising more rapidly than elsewhere on Earth, what consequences might this have?

Volcanic activity

Erupting volcanoes spew tremendous amounts of particulate matter and sulfur gases (which form sulfur aerosols) into the atmosphere. These particulates and aerosols shield the Earth from solar radiation by reflecting incoming light back into space. Most volcanic eruptions therefore have a short-term cooling effect at the Earth's surface. However, very large eruptions may initiate a positive feedback effect that could amplify a cooling trend that was already underway.

Changes in concentrations of greenhouse gases

Analysis of air bubbles in ice cores has revealed a strong correlation between temperature and atmospheric CO_2 over the past 420,000 years (see graph), but it cannot describe for us the mechanisms of past fluctuations. A temperature-driven model might suggest that during warmer periods the level of CO_2 went up because the respiration rate of plants and soil bacteria increased. An atmosphere-driven model might suggest that high concentrations of CO_2 led to warming by enhancing the natural greenhouse effect. While we may never answer such chicken-and-egg questions about the past, it is increasingly clear that human activities that increase greenhouse gases — especially the burning of fossil fuels and deforestation — are responsible for the climate changes observed and predicted at present. ❧

Atmospheric Carbon Dioxide and Temperature Change, 420,000 years ago to Present

Parts per Million Volume — Degrees Celsius

Carbon Dioxide Concentration

Temperature Change — Source: ORNL, Scripps

Thousand Years Ago

(World Resources Institute, *State of the World 2001*)

Gail Littlejohn is co-editor of Green Teacher *magazine in Toronto, Ontario.*

References

Francis, Jane E. "The Dynamics of Polar Fossil Forests: Tertiary Fossil Forests of Axel Heiberg Island, Canadian Arctic Archipelago." Geological Survey of Canada, *Bulletin 403*, 1991, pp. 29-38.

Pielou, E.C. *After the Ice Age: The Return of Life to Glaciated North America.* Chicago: University of Chicago Press, 1991.

Raven, Peter H., Evert, Ray F. and Eichorn, Susan E. *Biology of Plants*, 5th edition. New York: Worth Publishers, 1992.

Stephen Birch Aquarium Museum. *Forecasting the Future: Exploring Evidence for Global Climate Change.* Arlington, VA: National Science Teachers Association, 1996.

Is Climate Change Good for Us?

An activity for exploring how changes in climate could affect daily life and influence the economy of a region

by Jackie Oblak

To many people, the thought of temperatures rising two or three degrees Celsius does not seem to be a big deal, and to those who live in areas with cold winters it may even sound appealing. Yet global climate change brings with it a number of uncertainties about how regions will be affected. This activity is designed to encourage students to consider how changes in climate could affect them personally. They are then asked to broaden their focus by looking at the big picture to see how changes could affect their regions, whether they live in a rural or urban community, in the interior or along a coastline.

Although this activity is designed as an introductory exercise for primary and junior students, it can be easily modified for other levels by increasing the depth of the classroom discussion and research requirements. The exercise should serve as a reminder that even with our advanced technologies, we are dependent on the Earth's natural systems.

Background

We live in a world in which we expect a certain amount of climatic predictability. In temperate interior regions, we expect very warm summers and cold winters. In more southerly regions and along coastlines, we expect more rainfall in certain seasons than in others. For some, snow in May is typical; for others, annual droughts are the norm. Regardless of where we live, we have adapted our activities, economies and communities to seasonal cycles and climatic conditions which we have come to depend on.

One of the most important examples of our dependence on predictable weather patterns is found in agriculture. Plants have specific tolerances to rainfall, drought, and high and low temperatures, as well as to a number

Tom Goldsmith

of other variables. As a result, farmers rely on having predictable seasonal weather patterns when they determine what type of crops they will grow and when they will plant them. Many other businesses rely on the weather as well. Tourist attractions, ski operations, theme parks and camping facilities all depend on a number of optimal days, whether they be snow days or sun days, to stay in business. Think of how empty the beaches would be without the hot sunny days of summer, or how empty the ski hills would be if it rained most of the winter! Restaurants, hotels, transportation companies and other enterprises depend on these weather-reliant businesses to bring in customers.

The design of buildings within a region is also based on an expected range of weather conditions. In areas with high winds, for example, new buildings are constructed in such a way that they can be expected to withstand these winds. Flood-control dams are designed to handle a maximum amount of runoff within a certain period. Areas around rivers and lakes are often designated as being within in the "100-year plan," meaning that according to past trends, the area has only a one percent chance of flooding each year. Land use decisions depend on these designations and, like agriculture and tourism, are based on a certain amount of predictability in the weather. Major changes in weather patterns, such as large increases in rainfall, especially over a very short period of time, may increase the potential of flooding in these areas.

We tend to take it for granted that climate will stay the same within certain limits of variability; but if our climate does change, many other aspects of our lives could also change. Consider the occurrence of a hot, dry summer with many sunny days in a region that usually experiences rain about once a week. It may be great for us to have more sunny days than normal during summer vacation, but if there is more sun, there is potential for increased evaporation of moisture from the soil. Would farmers likely benefit from these wonderful sunny days? How might the resulting decline in crop yields affect the price and availability of food? What could happen if these weather conditions continued for a number of years? These are the types of details that this activity encourages students to consider when looking at climate change.

We tend to take for granted that climate will stay the same, within certain limits of variability; if it does change, many other aspects of our lives could also change.

Activity

This activity can be done individually, but students will benefit from discussing their ideas in groups.

1. Using the chart (see next page) as a starting point, have students discuss and record what they think would be the consequences of various climate changes. Note that the chart is very general, and does not expect the students to quantify the changes, but only to consider general trends. You may want to add other weather conditions or events that are common in your region. The following are examples of ideas that you might expect from primary or junior students:

Season: Summer

Type of Change: More rainstorms

How would this affect me?

~ My baseball and soccer games are likely to be cancelled more often.

~ Water may leak into our basement.

~ The storm spillways will fill with water and it may be dangerous to go near them.

~ The wind that comes with rainstorms may break branches on the large old trees near my house.

How would this affect things around me?

~ Local tomato farmers may have their crops ruined by hail or flooding of the fields. Tomato plants need regular rainfall with periods of sunshine. More storms may make the tomatoes crack and rot.

~ The local summer festival may not make as much money because more events will be rained out and fewer people will attend.

2. Once the groups have completed the chart, discuss the responses as a class. Ask if there are any categories in which there seem to be no negative effects. Remind students to consider the effects of storms and other events on infrastructures such as drainage, roads, electricity and so on.

3. What adaptations would humans have to make if certain weather events became more common? This can be approached as a "What if?" brainstorming exercise, or students may contact local climatologists to ask about actual trends and long-term predictions for your area. Adaptations considered might include modifications to infrastructure and buildings; and changes in diet, dress, activities and transportation.

Extensions

1. Have students research the climatic tolerances and potential effects of climate change on a local crop or natural resource. Information to be gathered might include the maximum and minimum amounts of rainfall and the range of temperatures that the crop tolerates, the number of frost-free days it requires for maturation, and its susceptibility to weather-influenced pests such as insects and fungus. Compare these tolerances to the local norms for your area (obtain charts showing annual precipitation, temperature, and sun days from local weather offices). In areas where a specific crop or resource is the cornerstone of the local economy, consider the economic, social and environmental consequences of lower harvests due to climate change (e.g., many people might lose their jobs; if people have less money to spend, local businesses will suffer; if local crops suffer, more food may have to be imported to the region, resulting in higher prices and greater consumption of fossil fuel).

2. How could changes in climate affect wildlife? Choose two or three species of insects, plants or animals and consider whether and how they would be affected. Since all organisms depend on other things in their habitat, encourage students to look at requirements for food, shelter and water, as well as interdependence with other organisms. How might changes in climate influence these factors?

3. The media frequently report extreme weather events that cause difficulties for individuals and local economies. Choose a current weather-related event and have the students identify the cause (e.g., rain for three weeks in a region that usually has rain once a month) and the result (e.g., mudslides, flooding of rivers, loss of life, houses, crops, safe drinking water).

4. Have students select several different regions of the world, including their own, and identify features of architecture, dress, diet and culture that may have developed as adaptations to the climate.

Evaluation
At the end of the exercise, the students should show an understanding that climate changes which many individuals may consider desirable (more sun, more time on the beach) may not be good for farmers, other sectors of the economy or other organisms. Students should also understand that we depend on natural systems to be relatively predictable and to function within certain limits. Students should be able to identify, in general terms, what could occur to local structures such as dams and storm sewers if climate were to be more severe than expected within a certain time period. ❧

Jackie Oblak is an environmental educator at the Bill Mason Centre of the Ottawa-Carleton District School Board in Ottawa, Ontario.

Season: _____		
Type of Climate Change	**How would it affect me?**	**How would it affect things around me?**
More rainstorms or snowstorms		
Less rainfall or snowfall		
More sunshine		
Less sunshine		
Higher daytime temperatures		
Lower daytime temperatures		
Higher wind speeds		
Other changes		

Energy: Making the Right Choices

The energy choices we make now may affect the Earth's climate for generations to come. In this practical unit, young students explore and assess the pros and cons of different sources of energy used by humans over time.

by Kitty Cochrane

It's haunting to watch the moon set from my classroom window on dark December mornings. Fort McMurray is a northern Alberta city which in the last two decades has boomed from 3,000 to 40,000 people. There are deep deposits of sand here, rich with black bitumen which is processed into fossil fuels. We are all in this dark, cold north because of it. The children arrive. The lights go on, the heat is turned up, the computer turned on, and the day's energy consumption begins. A lot of energy is used in the north — for warmth, light and transportation of goods that are unavailable locally. And a lot of energy is wasted here, too, as when people leave clouds of exhaust suspended in the frozen sky. Living here has made me realize how important it is that my grade two students learn to make wise energy choices.

The first step is for students to realize that people have always found energy to meet their needs. We brainstorm things they think they could not do if they lived in a world without electricity, and talk about what needs those things meet, such as a need for transportation, food, entertainment and shelter. What would people in places or times without electricity use to meet these needs? With help from *National Geographic*,

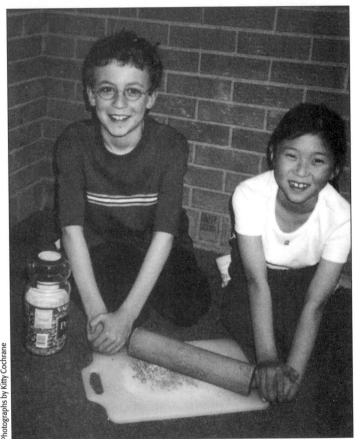

Making peanut butter by hand builds muscles and produces no pollution.

Photographs by Kitty Cochrane

we take a thorough look at humans using their own energy. Students use their own energy on tasks that for them are unusual, such as carrying water on their heads, and making butter by shaking cream in a jar until it congeals. They spin their own yarn on drop spindles made by poking a pencil through a potato. (Tie a string to the pencil tip at the bottom of the potato, twist the string around the other end of the pencil, twirl the potato, and twist raw wool onto the string.) Once they understand that humans have historically supplied their needs with their own energy, I take them onto the second step: understanding why we choose other energy sources.

We do a comparison between using electricity (a blender with peanuts and oil) and using human energy (peanuts and a rolling pin and bread board) to make peanut butter. I ask them to make a good/bad list on using human energy. Using their own energy makes them feel good about themselves and what they produce, gives them a chance to work and chat together, gives them more skills, makes them stronger, and produces no pollution. The bad points are that they get very tired, it takes a lot longer, it would keep them from doing important things (like go to school or play), they wouldn't be able to make as much money because they can do less, and using other humans to do the work might not be a fair thing (as in slavery and child labor).

As a third step we explore what people started using to help them do their work, the renewable energies. We again look at pictures of other places and times to identify how animal energy helps humans do work. We look at pictures of people gathering and using wood for cooking and heating. Students use wind energy to move a piece of paper on their desks without touching it, and make paper pinwheels mounted on straws. For water energy, they glue styrofoam egg-carton cups suspended on a pencil to make a simple water wheel. For solar energy we use solar-cell calculators. A lidded jar in a window, with a thermometer inside and a thermometer outside, shows passive solar energy through the rise of temperature inside the jar. We cook hot dogs on solar cookers fashioned from a tinfoiled shoe box set in the sun, with the wiener suspended on a coat hook piercing through the box.

As with human energy, we look at the good and bad points of each of the renewable energies. Wood energy can be grown again, but causes air pollution and depletes our world's forests, which in turn affects rain patterns. Solar and wind energy are pollutant-free, but hard to store, and cannot be used in areas that are not sunny or windy. Water energy is constant, but building huge dams forces people to leave their lands and interferes with salmon spawning.

For the fourth step, I explain that as people started using more machines and factories, they also used more electricity, supplied by fossil fuels. We handle charcoal and discuss coal fuel. Our hands become black as we break it open, and we talk about the danger to people who dig up coal, breathe in coal dust, and get caught in mine disasters. Weather permitting, we go outside and burn the coal, watching the smoke rise and talking about global warming (another comparison can be set up using coal and a solar cooker to cook hot dogs). We talk about the pollution created in finding and digging up fossil fuels, in converting fossil fuels into something we can use, and the final pollution caused by using it (gas, oil) or throwing it out (plastics). Their homework is to put

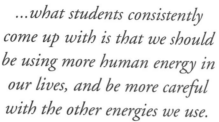

...what students consistently come up with is that we should be using more human energy in our lives, and be more careful with the other energies we use.

Students create a stir exploring the use of human energy to make butter.

gas in a car, and to put a kleenex over the exhaust pipe of a running vehicle for five minutes to see evidence of the pollutants released through the burning of fossil fuels. We talk about fossil fuel being precious because not every country has it, yet everyone wants it. The 1991 Persian Gulf War is a reminder that people actually fight wars over fossil fuels. Again they summarize all the bad things about using fossil fuel and coal energy (human lives lost, pollution, wars), and the good things (it's cheap, easy and available).

To help students summarize and put into action their learning, I give them three World Energy Problems:

1) The energy that is being used the most causes the most pollution.
2) The world's richest people are hogging the world's energy.
3) The use of wood energy is causing our forests to be destroyed.

Each group tackles one problem, talking about why that problem exists and what they can do to help, starting today. It's a deep thinking exercise for young children, but it is enchanting to see them articulate to each other their understanding of energy consumption and its ramifications. And what they consistently come up with is that we should be using more human energy in our lives, and be more careful with the other energies we use. They make a list of ways they are going to change their habits so they use less energy. And they decide on how they can share what they've learned with one new person.

I come away from this unit entranced with how young children can gain such a thorough understanding of such a huge and important issue. And I find it reaffirming to see them tackling energy issues with a clear belief in what is needed and possible, and an obvious commitment to making it happen. ✸

Kitty Cochrane teaches at Dickinsfield School in Fort McMurray, Alberta.

Introducing Solar Electricity

Hands-on activities to familiarize students with solar technology

by Robert Vogl and Sonia Vogl

Since the dawn of time, humans have looked to the sun as the source of light and warmth. Yet it is only in the past few decades that we have learned to use the sun's energy for the ultimate source of power: electricity that is virtually free and non-polluting and that will last as long as the Earth. Solar energy technologies have been steadily improving since their emergence in the early 1970s, and advocates of solar electricity believe that its widespread adoption in both home and industry is within reach. But as with any new technology, if solar electricity is to gain public acceptance, people will have to become more familiar with it.

For the classroom teacher, finding interesting ways to present the topic of solar electricity is challenging. While solar electricity has an intellectual appeal, the lack of moving parts and the silent operation of solar installations may fail to sustain students' interest, and simply viewing solar-powered appliances such as yard lights is a non-participatory learning experience. Recognizing these problems, we have developed hands-on activities to help students understand the technology and some of its applications, and to encourage them to use solar-powered devices in their own lives and to advocate its wider acceptance in society.

The following is a selection of activities that can be used to introduce solar electricity to students in middle grades and up. Students begin by acquiring a basic understanding of how a solar panel works and how its energy can be stored. They then learn how to use solar electricity to power appliances and investigate the applications of the technology in their community.

Sonia Vogl

Students practice orienting a solar panel to power small appliances.

How solar electricity is produced

Solar cells are made primarily of silicon, an element that reacts well as a semi-conductor. When photons, or packets of energy from the sun, bombard the silicon, some photons hit the electrons in the outer orbit of silicon atoms. If a photon's energy level is similar to that of the electron it hits, the electron will capture the energy of the photon and move out of the silicon into the circuit. The movement of many electrons is the flow of electricity. If the photon does not have enough energy to move the electron, it simply passes through the silicon; if it has too much energy, the excess is released as heat.

Many young people are already familiar with electronic gadgets based on semi-conductors. Their lives are filled with the solid state technologies used in radios, stereos, televisions and personal computers. Solar cells are merely another application of this technology.

Solar simulation

Students will more easily understand the production of solar electricity if they can visualize it by participating in a simulation of the process. In this activity, one student plays the role of the sun, four students play the role of the four electrons in the outer ring of a silicon atom, and several other students play the role of appliances installed along an electrical circuit.

To begin, draw a circle about 1.5 meters (4') in diameter. The four "electrons" stand on this circle, simulating the four electrons in the outer ring of a silicon atom. Next, create a "circuit" by drawing a large oval chalk line about 5 meters long and 2 meters wide (15' x 6') outside of the electron circle. The student who represents the sun holds several soft balls which represent photons, or packets of energy from the sun. The sun tosses the balls, one at a time, to the electrons. When an

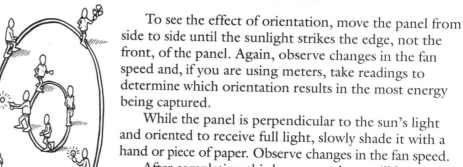

electron catches a ball, it becomes "energized" and runs through the electrical circuit and back into the outer ring of the silicon atom. The electron then releases excess energy by tossing the ball to the teacher. Along the line that represents the circuit, other students can play the roles of appliances such as a light bulb, fan or buzzer. As the electrons pass by them, the appliances whirl or buzz to indicate that they are powered on.

This activity can be made more complex to fit the abilities of the class, but the basic activity will "turn on the light" for most students.

Orienting and using a solar panel

Work with solar panels, voltage meters and small appliances introduces students to the production and use of solar electricity. It also affords an opportunity to review basic concepts of electricity such as volts (force that causes the electrons to flow), amps (rate of flow of electrons), watts (combined volts and amps), and circuits. The following simple activity demonstrates that a solar panel should be perpendicular to the sun's light and should receive full sun in order to capture the most energy.

For this activity, you will need solar panels, small appliances such as low-wattage fans or lights, and, if available, a voltmeter (measures voltage) and ammeter (measures amperage) for taking precise readings of energy output. Small solar panels and appliances may be purchased from a hobby shop that carries electronic equipment or from a science and technology supply house. The appliances should be sized to the solar panel; for example, if the panel produces one watt of electricity, the appliance should use one watt of electricity.

The inclination of a solar panel refers to its vertical (north-south) angle, while its orientation refers to its east-west angle. To observe the effect of inclination, connect the panel to the appliance (in this example, a fan) and position the panel perpendicular to the sun's rays. Observe the speed of the fan and, if using meters, read and record the voltage and amps in the circuit. Slowly move the panel so that it is inclined horizontally, then continue moving the panel until it is vertical. Observe the speed of the fan; it should slow down whenever the panel is off the perpendicular position.

To see the effect of orientation, move the panel from side to side until the sunlight strikes the edge, not the front, of the panel. Again, observe changes in the fan speed and, if you are using meters, take readings to determine which orientation results in the most energy being captured.

While the panel is perpendicular to the sun's light and oriented to receive full light, slowly shade it with a hand or piece of paper. Observe changes in the fan speed.

After completing this lesson, students will have acquired the basic concepts necessary for calculating the size of a simple solar electric system. As a follow-up activity, challenge them to calculate the number of solar panels they would need to run appliances in an installation such as a cabin. For example, four 15-watt lights would require a total output of 60 watts, or one 12-volt panel that produces 5 amps.

Storing electricity

A major concern when using solar electricity is that appliances need to run after dark and on cloudy days. This requires that the electricity produced during sunny periods be stored for later use. The following activities demonstrate that batteries and hydrogen gas can both be used to store solar electricity.

Storing energy in batteries: The most common method of storing solar electricity is to use it to charge batteries. For a classroom demonstration, small batteries such as size "AA" can be charged in a relatively short time. Use only rechargeable batteries and ensure that their power has been drawn down. Either place the batteries in a readily available battery holder or use a pre-made solar battery charger. Connect the positive end of the batteries to the positive side of the solar panel and the negative end of the batteries to the negative side of the panel. Place the solar panel and batteries in full sunlight for a day. Test the batteries in an appliance such as a small radio.

Keep your solar battery charger on hand in the classroom throughout the year so that students can charge and recharge batteries for use at home. This is one simple means of increasing awareness of solar electricity as a viable way to produce electricity in daily life.

Storing energy as hydrogen: Solar electricity can be used to split water molecules into hydrogen and oxygen, a process that allows the sun's energy to be stored as hydrogen for later use. The ability to isolate hydrogen gas is one of the basic principles behind the hydrogen fuel cell being developed as an alternative to fossil fuels for powering automobiles. The energy produced in hydrogen fuel cells comes from the bonding of hydrogen with oxygen, a reaction in which energy is released and water is formed.

The following activity demonstrates the use of solar electricity to split water molecules into hydrogen gas and oxygen gas. Two students should work together for this experiment. Each pair of students will need a small container such as a 500 ml (1 pint) plastic carton, two small prescription bottles, two 30 cm (12") lengths of bare wire, a pencil, two alligator clamps, water, washing soda, a solar panel, and a match. The solar panel must produce at least three volts for this to work.

1. Tightly coil 20 cm (8") of each piece of wire by wrapping it around a pencil.
2. Fill the container with warm water and dissolve 30 grams (1 ounce) of washing soda in the water. (The soda speeds up the reaction.)
3. Place the pill bottles in the container and let them fill with water. While they are under water, insert the coiled ends of the wires into them.
4. Carefully move the bottles so that they are upside down under water.
5. Connect the remaining ends of the wires to the solar panel using alligator clamps.
6. Set the panel in full sunlight. Observe as bubbles appear in the bottles. Since hydrogen has one extra electron, it has a negative charge and will collect at the positive wire. Oxygen lacks the extra electron, so it will collect at the negative wire.

In as little time as ten minutes, the bottle connected to the positive pole of the panel will be filled with hydrogen gas. To demonstrate that it is hydrogen, have students work in pairs to flame it off. One student carefully covers the open end of the bottle with a finger and lifts it from the water. It is important to keep the bottle upside down; hydrogen is lighter than air and will remain in the bottle in this position. The second student lights the match and holds it above the bottle of hydrogen. The first student then turns the bottle upright so that its opening is directly under the lighted match. The hydrogen gas will flow upward and a small pop will be heard as it burns. This characteristic pop is an indication that the gas that collected in the bottle was indeed hydrogen.

As a follow-up, encourage interested students to investigate fuel cell technology and its present and potential applications in daily life.

Designing with solar electricity

To demonstrate a simple application of solar electricity, use solar panels to power battery-driven toys such as walkie-talkies and toy trucks (connect the toys to the panel using alligator clamps). Be sure to select toys that use the same amount of power that your panel produces. As an individual or a group project, have students create and test their own solar-powered toys or appliances.

Many educators are enthusiastic supporters of competitions in which students race small solar-powered cars [see "Solar Car Sprints," page 28]. Advanced students can be involved in the design of the cars as well as the race, while younger students can assemble cars using predesigned kits.

Local uses of solar electricity

Discovering local uses of solar electricity will help students become more aware of the practical applications of this technology. Begin by having students brainstorm a list of solar-powered devices they have seen or used, such as calculators, watches and flashlights. Then assign teams to survey different blocks of the community, looking for solar installations such as sidewalk lights or rooftop panels on dwellings. For each installation, the team should record the address and specific use (if obvious) and, if possible, take photographs which can be used to create an informative school display. Follow up by interviewing or sending surveys to people who own solar electric applications. Questions might include: Why did you choose solar electricity? What do you use it for? How is it working? What impact, if any, has it had on your energy bills? Be sure to ask whether those interviewed or surveyed would be willing to talk to the class about solar electricity.

Solar groundhogs

We have sponsored a solar version of the weather-predicting prowess of groundhogs by having students measure solar output in amps and then predict how many days of winter remain. While no more scientific than a groundhog's prediction, it can add some fun to collecting solar data and sharing it with others. It can also serve to alert students to solar cycles and signs of changing weather patterns.

Conclusions

The transition to a clean and more optimistic energy future is underway, but there is still much resistance and inertia inherent in our society's reliance on fossil fuels. Young people are important sources of the ideas and inspiration that will be essential in overcoming this inertia. If we can help students appreciate and learn to work with solar electricity, this non-polluting and virtually free energy direct from the sun could well be the most promising energy source for our future. ❦

Robert Vogl and Sonia Vogl recently retired from Northern Illinois University. They have taught environmental education for over 35 years and solar electricity for over ten years.

Solar Box Cooking

A tasty introduction to the practical use of passive solar energy

by Sue LeBeau

Thousands of years ago the Greeks and Romans realized that the sun is the great source of heat and light in our world. They designed their homes and cities so that all could benefit from its inexhaustible energy. The sun was at the heart of their lives. Today we take for granted the energy we receive from the sun, and many students are truly not aware that it is the original energy source for all of our daily activities. A flick of the switch gives us light; a turn of the thermostat gives us warmth for our homes; a twist of the knob gives us heat for cooking our food. For most of these activities we are burning fossil fuels and contributing to the rising levels of greenhouse gases in the Earth's atmosphere.

Once students understand the environmental effects of burning of fossil fuels, the next step is to ask: What can we do about it? How can we meet our needs for light and heat without creating pollution? While students are well aware that the sun is a source of light, few in most cases have discovered the adventure of using the energy of sunlight for the everyday task of cooking. Making and using a solar box cooker to prepare favorite foods such as hot dogs, cookies and pizza is a fun, practical way to experience the possibilities of capturing the sun's energy for our daily needs. A solar box cooker is simply a shallow container with an aluminum foil interior, a glass or plexiglass top, and a reflector lid. The theory behind the cooker is simple: to concentrate and trap the energy of the sun in a container long enough to cook food.

Most solar box cookers are so simple they can be built by children, and there are many different ways to construct one. Once students have seen a basic design (see page 26), they may be able to think of ways in which the oven may be improved. Encourage them with questions such as: Which type of oven would work better, shallow or deep? Would it help to insulate the oven? Would painting or covering the outside with a certain color improve the oven? Would adding more reflectors help? What about a totally different design? (You may want to suggest using a cardboard pizza box or a potato chip can with a silver metallic interior.) Have students implement their ideas in the construction of their own models. Using oven thermometers to measure the temperature, hold a contest to see which model heats up fastest or reaches the highest temperature. You can expect temperatures of 110°-165°C (200°-300°F) in the model shown. By experimenting with the design (e.g., adding more reflectors), students may be able to capture more light and, hence, more heat.

The most fun of all comes when you actually cook food. Try simple things first, such as cookies, hot dogs or nachos, and then have students try different recipes and experiment further. What cooks best in the solar cooker? Will food cook more quickly if it is in a black container? Does a lightweight container, such as an enamelled steel pot or a coffee can, work better than a

Photographs by Sue LeBeau

Top: Cookies baking in a solar box cooker. Bottom: Students combine imagination and principles of solar energy to produce an eclectic variety of solar cookers.

Making a simple solar box cooker

THIS SIMPLE SOLAR COOKER provides a practical way to demonstrate solar power. Sunlight goes through the top window and reflects off shiny walls onto black surfaces where it changes to heat.

Materials:

- Two cardboard boxes, one small enough to fit inside the other leaving a gap of 5 to 7 cm (about 2-3") between the boxes. The inner box should be about 48 cm x 58 cm x 20 cm (19" x 23" x 8").

- A flat piece of cardboard about 20 cm (8") longer and wider than the large box.

- Glass or plexiglass (clear mylar) for a window about 50 cm x 60 cm (20" x 24"). The glass should be slightly bigger than the smallest box.

- A thin black metal tray or cardboard painted black, to go inside the smaller box.

- Newspaper for insulation.

- About 2.5 to 3 meters (8-10 ft) of heavy-duty aluminum foil.

- Masking tape or water-based glue to fasten the foil to the boxes and to tape the edge of the glass to protect it.

- Dark cooking pots with lids.

Procedure:

1. Cover with foil. Cover the following surfaces with aluminum foil: the inside and outside of the small box, the inside of the large box, and one side of the flat piece of cardboard. The foil can be secured with masking tape or with water-based glue that is diluted and applied with a brush.

2. Assemble and insulate. Put the small box inside the larger one and stuff crumpled newspaper or other non-toxic insulating material between the walls so the boxes rest snugly. Do not insulate with styrofoam as it may emit toxic fumes when heated. Fold down the walls so they are all the same height.

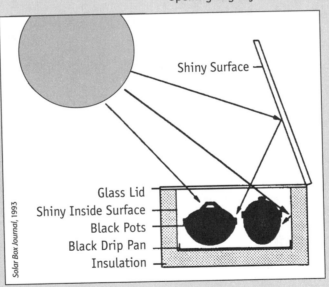

Shiny Surface

Glass Lid
Shiny Inside Surface
Black Pots
Black Drip Pan
Insulation

Solar Box Journal, 1993

3. Make a lid. Center the flat piece of cardboard, foil side down, on top of the assembled box. Fold down the 10 cm (4") of cardboard that hangs over the edges, make cuts at the corners, and fold and glue the edges. In the top of the lid, cut three sides of a rectangle to create a reflective flap and an opening slightly smaller than the glass.

4. Install the glass. Fit the glass over the innermost box so there are no large air leaks. Another method is to turn the lid upside down and glue or tape the plexiglass to its inner edges to form a lid with a window.

5. Finishing touches: Place the thin black metal tray (or black-painted cardboard) on the bottom of the smaller box. Using a coat hanger or stick, make a prop to hold up the reflective flap on the lid.

6. Start cooking! Place the box outside on a dry surface that will be sunny for several hours. Put food in covered black pots and place the pots toward the back of the cooker. Fit the lid snugly on the cooker.

To get the most from the sun, start cooking in mid-morning. Aim the box so the lid reflector will face the sun in late morning or early afternoon, and position the reflector so that it shines light into the inner box. You may want to tip the cooker a little to catch the most sunlight.

heavy cast iron pot? What if the food is in smaller pieces? How often should the cooker be refocused to catch maximum light as the sun passes overhead? The opportunities for experimentation are endless.

Once students realize that cooking with sunlight is both easy and fun, capitalize on this enthusiasm by holding "sun bake-offs" or "solar-cues." Invite other students and staff to experience the sun's cooking power by sharing your sun-cooked foods. Students may also wish to raise money for environmental causes or projects by selling their solar snacks. But the heart of the lesson should center on how the use of solar energy helps the environment. Cooking with sunlight is economical and pollution-free. There's no fuel to buy, there are no trees to cut down, it does not create a fire hazard and there are no ashes to clean up.

How often you are able to use your solar box cooker depends on how much sunshine you get in your part of the world. The topic of "solar geography" can itself lead to investigation and discussion. Have older students research and map the amount of solar radiation received in various parts of the world. This should lead them to discover that many parts of Africa, Asia and Latin America receive abundant sunshine. Half of the world's families live in these regions and most depend on wood to cook their food. In many areas, trees are being cut for fuel more quickly than they can be replanted, leading to soil erosion, loss of wildlife habitat, local air pollution, and the emission of greenhouse gases. A solar cooker can be used year-round in the tropics and can cut a family's use of wood in half, thus saving forests, drastically reducing local air pollution, and relieving people from the daily burden of

> "If only 1% of the 1.5 billion people affected by cooking fuel shortages today were to use solar cookers seven months a year, they would save two million tons of wood. This would prevent the release of 85,000 tons of pollutants and save the equivalent of 10 million trees a year."
>
> **— Joseph Radabaugh, *Heaven's Flame***

travelling long distances to gather firewood. Students can share their knowledge of solar cookers by becoming "sun pals" with kids from a developing nation. For example, my students exchanged letters and photos with several classes from The Gambia in west Africa. Besides forming lifelong friendships, the students raised money to send solar box cookers to their friends' village. Such experiences are truly global and most unforgettable.

Solar energy is what makes life possible on Earth. Just as the Greeks and Romans did long ago, many today are turning to the sun as a source of clean, renewable energy. There's much that solar energy can do already and much more still to be discovered. Just maybe one of your students will be the scientist who makes one of those discoveries. ❧

Sue LeBeau teaches fifth grade at the West End School in Long Branch, New Jersey.

North American students raised money to send this solar box cooker to their "sun pals" in west Africa. Using the sun's energy to boil water and cook meals has enormous health and environmental benefits in tropical villages where wood is the only other fuel.

Resources for teaching about solar cooking

Arizona Energy Office. *A Day in the Sun*, 1991, video. This 18-minute video filmed at a solar cookout in Tucson, Arizona, shows a range of solar cooker technologies and a variety of foods being cooked. Arizona Energy Office, 3800 North Central, S-1200, Phoenix, AZ 85012, (602) 280-1402.

Halacy, Beth and Dan. *Cooking With The Sun: How to Build and Use Solar Cookers.* Lafayette, CA: Morning Sun Press, 1992, 114 pages, ISBN 0-96290-69-2-1. Available in Canada from Advance School Equipment, PO Box 488, Ponoka, AB T4J 1S8, (800) 465-7737 (part #52158); in the U.S. from Pitsco, PO Box 1708, Pittsburg, KS 66762, (800) 835-0686.

Radabaugh, Joseph. *Heaven's Flame: A Guide to Solar Cookers.* Ashland, Oregon: Home Power Publishing, 1998, 144 pages, ISBN 0-9629588-2-4, from Home Power, PO Box 275, Ashland, OR 97520, (800) 707-6585 or (541) 512-0201. A knowledgeable and companionable overview of solar cookers in use around the world, and step-by-step instructions for building and using simple yet effective cookers with inexpensive and recycled materials.

Solar Cookers International is a non-profit organization that promotes solar cooking as a solution to deforestation in developing countries. SCI sponsors a Solar Cooking Archive at http://solarcooking.org and has the following publications: *Solar Cooking Primer, How to Make Solar Cookers,* a Teachers' Kit, and a cookbook, *Solar Cooking Naturally.* Solar Cookers International, 1919 21st St., S-101, Sacramento, CA 95814, (916) 455-4499.

Solar Car Sprints

*Building and racing solar-powered cars is a fun way for
middle years students to learn about renewable energy*

by Aisling O'Shea

It has been called the modern-day Pinewood Derby, but whereas the Boy Scouts of the past built their cars of old-fashioned wood, the principal component of these cars is the photovoltaic cell. Junior Solar Sprint is a program in which middle years students design, build and race model cars powered only by solar energy. The program begins in the classroom where teachers and mentors from the science and engineering communities work with students as they design and build the cars while learning about solar energy and engineering. It ends on the race track, where students compete — from the school level all the way up to the national level — with the cars they have built.

Junior Solar Sprint was created in 1989 by Argonne National Laboratory as a means of introducing students to science and engineering in a hands-on way. The project is supported by the United States Department of Energy and coordinated by volunteers across the country. While students of all ages enjoy building Junior Solar Sprint cars, racing them on the competitive level is limited to those in grades six through eight. Each contestant begins with a kit containing a three-volt photovoltaic panel and a motor. With certain provisions (for example, each car must carry a payload of an empty pop can), the design of the car is up to the students' imaginations. Cars at Junior Solar Sprint competitions are judged on speed, technical merit, craftsmanship and innovation, providing a number of ways for students to excel.

The program can be introduced into schools as an extracurricular activity; as part of the physics, Earth science, technical or transportation curricula; or as a cross-curricular project. One of the best things about Junior Solar Sprint is that it encourages learning in many different disciplines. Manipulating gears and experimenting with aerodynamic principles is a great introduction to physics, while designing the cars ties in closely with both art and technical education, as cars are judged on their artistic and technical merit as well as the care with which they are built. Junior Solar Sprint can also be incorporated into math class where statistics and graphing can be used to chart progress and show ideas

Solar car competitions foster teamwork, multidisciplinary learning, and the exhilaration of finding solutions to technical problems.

for improvement. In history class, students can study the history of energy, particularly renewable energy (from the worship of the sun by the ancient Egyptians through the oil crisis of the 1970s to current progress in fuel-cell, wind and solar technologies). In English class, students can write reports on solar energy as well as essays about their experiences with Junior Solar Sprint. In social studies, students can examine current issues related to energy choices, and the social and economic costs and benefits of various renewable energy options. These learning opportunities help to make Junior Solar Sprint not merely an add-on to a science unit, but rather an educational event that travels across curriculum boundaries.

Another important educational aspect of Junior Solar Sprint is its promotion of cooperative learning. Students build cars in teams, typically in groups of two to four. This teamwork not only reduces the number of kits needing to be purchased, but also helps to compensate for individual weaknesses and draw out personal strengths to produce the best car possible. Important cooperative learning also occurs through the mentor system. While teachers usually act as coaches for the teams, often the mentors are local scientists and engineers. This mentoring by professionals gives kids a chance to interact with adults other than their parents or teachers and encourages them to engage in the project as scientists in their own right.

While the Junior Solar Sprint program can be undertaken without participating in races, the competitive aspect introduces an element of fun to the proceedings (Junior Solar Sprint races tend to resemble carnivals more than they do scientific experiments). The racing season typically begins in February, when interested

It is one thing to be told that photovoltaics is the direct conversion of sunlight to electricity, but quite another to see a car that you built yourself running on sunlight.

teachers and mentors meet with area coordinators. School and town races are held in the early spring, area races in mid-May, regional championships in mid-June and the nationals take place at the end of the summer. Being involved in a Junior Solar Sprint race is a worthwhile experience for anyone, from the contestants themselves, to their teachers and mentors, to the volunteers who work on the program. The visible enthusiasm for science and engineering, the sound of "photovoltaics" rolling off the tongues of 12-year-olds, and the friendly com-

petition and sharing of ideas are clear demonstrations that Junior Solar Sprint is a perfect hands-on way to illustrate renewable energy to students. It is one thing to be told that photovoltaics is the direct conversion of sunlight to electricity, but quite another to see a car that you built yourself running solely on sunlight.

Students come away from the Junior Solar Sprint program having learned unforgettable lessons about renewable energy, mechanics and physics. They have expressed their creative impulses and developed problem-solving skills in the making of the cars. They have learned invaluable lessons in teamwork and cooperation. But perhaps most important, students come away with the satisfaction of having tackled a scientific problem and found their own solutions to it.

Speed counts, but cars are also judged on craftsmanship.

Junior Solar Sprint can be undertaken at any school, anywhere in the world. While competition is limited to middle schoolers, the building of model cars transcends age, and the associated activities can be adjusted as necessary. Once you obtain the kits, the program can be taken as far as you and your students wish to go with it — from a one-day class activity to an eight-week multidisciplinary unit to the national championships. The choice is yours, and the sun is waiting. ❧

Aisling O'Shea is an advisor to the board of directors of Solar Now, Inc. in Beverly, Massachusetts.

Getting Started in Junior Solar Sprint

FOR INFORMATION ABOUT JOINING OR INITIATING a Junior Solar Sprint in your area, contact:

Science and Technology Education Programs
National Renewable Energy Laboratory
1617 Cole Boulevard
Golden, CO 80401
Phone (303) 275-3044; in the U.S. (800) 639-3649

Website: Materials at the Junior Solar Sprint website include program information and rules, a Teacher and Mentor Guide, Student Guide, Classroom Investigations, and Tips on Construction. See www.nrel.gov/education/natjss.html.

Kits: A basic solar sprint kit contains a three-volt photovoltaic panel, motor and gears, and the rules of the race. Kits containing all car parts are also available. In Canada, order from Advance School Equipment, (800) 465-7737 or (403) 783-3777; for U.S. distributors, see www.nrel.gov/education/kits.

Renewable Energy: K-12 Activities

by Sue LeBeau

The following activities allow students to explore some of the renewable energy alternatives to the use of fossil fuels. They are divided into grade level categories but many can be adapted to several levels.

Grades K-3
Math

Shifting Shadows: Talk about why shadows are different lengths in the morning, midday and afternoon. Have students measure their shadows with partners at different times during the day and graph the results. Extend the activity throughout the year by comparing the lengths of shadows during different seasons.

Art

Energy Mobile: Initiate a class discussion about energy in general and renewable energy sources in particular. As each energy topic is introduced have students draw a picture that best illustrates for them that particular source of energy. Arrange the pictures to form energy mobiles to be displayed in the classroom.

Science

Sun Tea: Place water and tea bags in a jar with a lid and set it in the sun for three or four hours. Celebrate the sun's energy by serving your tea to special people in your school or just enjoy it yourselves! You may want to add sugar or lemon wedges.

Wind Energy: Begin a discussion about wind energy by having the students share their experiences of being in the wind. What places are very windy? Have they ever experienced a hurricane or tornado or severe wind storm? Illustrate the enormous power of the wind by having students make and fly kites or create pinwheels. Older students may make paper gliders and determine what variations of design will make them fly further.

Language Arts

Legends: Many stories, myths and legends relate the origin of the sun or the role the sun plays in our world. Read and discuss several of these with the students, pointing out the difference between fact and fiction. Some suggested books are: *Legends of the Sun and Moon* by Erice Hadley; *The Miser Who Wanted the Sun* by Jurg Obrist; and *Sun and Moon* by Marcus Pfister. Have students write their own "big book" class story about the sun's importance to our world or a legend about the sun's origin.

Grades 4-6
Science

Wind Energy: Wind is simply air in motion. The sun heats the air, the warm air rises and the cooler air flows in to take its place. At any given moment, half of the Earth's atmosphere is exposed to the sun and half is in shadow. This un-even heating and cooling creates wind. About two percent of the solar energy that falls on Earth is converted to wind energy. Wind can be used to generate electricity, 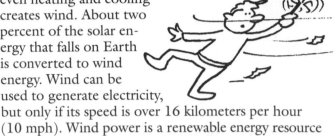 but only if its speed is over 16 kilometers per hour (10 mph). Wind power is a renewable energy resource that can provide clean, nonpolluting energy where wind is abundant and available on a regular basis. How much wind energy is available where you live? Have students build a device to measure wind speeds and discuss whether or not producing electricity through wind would be possible in your area. Conduct research to find which country is the world's leading wind-energy producer.

Art

Bumper Stickers: After discussing the benefits of using renewable energy, have students brainstorm slogans and create colorful bumper stickers that promote the use of various renewable energies. These may then be displayed on school bulletin boards, store windows or back windows of vehicles.

Language Arts

Alphabet Books: Read a number of science-oriented alphabet books with your students to serve as models for this activity. Suggested books: *The Desert Alphabet Book* by Jerry Pallotta; *A Swim Through the Sea* by Kristen Joy Pratt; and *The A,B,C of the Biosphere* by Professor Finch. Discuss with your students the characteristics and writing style of these books. Be sure to discuss the role that illustration plays. Have the students work in groups to create a "Renewable Energy Alphabet Book" that includes, defines and illustrates words related to renewable energy. Share the books with younger students.

Poetry: Have students create poems about renewable energy sources. Display the poems, with illustrations, on a bulletin board or compile them into a class book. Poems may be categorized by subject or by poetry style. As an alternative activity, write jingles, or new lyrics to familiar tunes, that carry a "renewable energy" theme.

Grades 7-9

Language Arts

Letters to the Editor: Discuss the purpose and characteristics of "Letters to the Editor" and read several such letters from your local newspaper. Then ask the students, either individually or in pairs, to write letters expressing their concern about the energy of the future and what should be done on the local and national levels to encourage a greater use of renewable energy today. Encourage students to send their letters to local newspapers for possible publication.

Math

Reducing Vehicle Emissions: Ask students to create a transportation log and collect data for one week on their families' transportation. Record the lengths and purposes of trips, fuel used, potential alternative modes of transportation, and any other information deemed important. Analyze and graph the collected data. Discuss ways that students and their families can reduce vehicle emissions and vehicle use in general. Publish a class list of "Ways to Reduce Emissions" and distribute it to students' families and other adults.

Geography

Geothermal: The word geothermal comes from the Greek words *geo* (earth) and *therme* (heat). Geothermal energy comes from the heat deep within the Earth. Some of the visible features of geothermal energy are volcanoes, hot springs and geysers; but most geothermal resources cannot be seen because they are deep underground. The Earth is a hotbed of geothermal energy. The most active geothermal resources are usually found along tectonic plate boundaries where earthquakes and volcanoes are concentrated. Most of the geothermal activity in the world occurs in an area called the "Ring of Fire" which rims the Pacific Ocean. Have students research ways of tapping this energy source, and create and label a world map showing the locations of the best known geothermal energy sources. Display maps and posters in the school.

Grades 10-12

Science and Technology

Biomass: Biomass is any organic matter — wood, animal wastes, crops, seaweed — that can be used as an energy source. It is probably our oldest source of energy and is still the main source for over half of the world's population. Investigate and create a model of this process and the technology used to generate electricity from it. Have students weigh the pros and cons of biomass as a source of energy and describe how biomass energy affects the environment.

Social Studies and Math

Graphic Results: The quantities and sources of energy used around the world vary from country to country. Ask students to choose at least three developing countries and three industrialized countries (including their own) and make a bar graph illustrating the annual per capita energy use. Create another graph that illustrates the sources of energy. Draw conclusions about the use of alternative sources of energy in these countries and share results with the class. Ask students to predict the future energy needs of these countries and make proposals for meeting those needs with the least environmental impact.

Research/Reporting

Hydropower:
Hydropower is energy that comes from the force of moving water. Hydropower is called a renewable energy source because it is replenished by snow and rainfall. A typical hydropower plant is a system with at least three parts: an electric plant, a dam and a reservoir.  Have students contact a local utility to inquire about the process of making electricity through hydropower. Further research should highlight: What role has hydropower played in electricity production in North America, past and present? What are the top hydropower-producing locations in the world today? How is solar power responsible for producing hydropower? How does hydropower affect the environment?

Performing Arts

The Future Is Now: Have students research and then create a skit that portrays a community or country that sees its fossil fuel supply dwindling and is concerned about meeting its future energy needs. The skit should include a plan for the future that highlights the use of one or more alternative energy sources.

Social Studies and Art

Editorial Cartoons: One of the ways in which the sun's energy can be changed into electricity is through photovoltaic conversion. Cars powered by photovoltaic cells would greatly reduce harmful emissions while conserving fossil fuels; however, at the present time, solar cars are costly to produce and require frequent "recharging." Have students create an editorial cartoon that reflects their opinion on whether or not research should continue on the solar powered car.

Sue LeBeau teaches fifth grade at the West End School in Long Branch, New Jersey.

A New Kind of Bus Afoot

Walking school buses — reducing carbon emissions the old-fashioned way

by Elise Houghton

Remember walking to school in your childhood? Until the 1970s most urban children went to school in environmentally-friendly, cost-efficient fashion — on foot. Along the way, they enjoyed the company of siblings and friends and a bit of healthy exercise. Twenty-five years ago, nearly 80 percent of grade three students in Canada walked or biked to school unaccompanied by adults. Today that figure is down to 10 percent.[1] In the United States, it is estimated that only 13 percent of students walk to school.[2] With traffic congestion growing in urban centers and concern about child molestation or abduction on the rise, more and more parents routinely drive their children even short distances to school. The results: social isolation, more car traffic, less vibrant (and often less safe) city streets, poorer air quality around schools, and reinforcement of the habits and attitudes that have made our society so dependent on fossil fuels and private automobiles.

A new movement is now afoot to reverse this trend. Following the lead of parent groups in Europe and Australia, more than a thousand schools in North America have initiated walk-to-school programs in recent years. Many have been inspired and assisted by national programs such as "Active and Safe Routes to School" in Canada and "Walk a Child to School" in the United States. At their fullest expression, walk-to-school programs focus on the following practical activities.

Greenest City

❧ Mapping the school neighborhood to determine the safest routes to and from school. As part of the social studies curriculum, students as young as seven years old participate by drawing maps and discussing the best routes for walking and cycling to school.

❧ Organizing "Walking (or Cycling) School Buses" led by parent "bus drivers" who take turns accompanying their own and neighboring children safely to and from school along set routes.

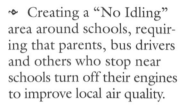

❧ Creating a "No Idling" area around schools, requiring that parents, bus drivers and others who stop near schools turn off their engines to improve local air quality.

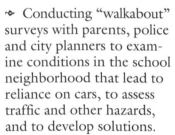

❧ Conducting "walkabout" surveys with parents, police and city planners to examine conditions in the school neighborhood that lead to reliance on cars, to assess traffic and other hazards, and to develop solutions.

❧ Participating in International Walk to School Day (IWALK) held each year in early October. This increasingly popular event honors walking school bus programs and exposes parents and children to the joys of walking. In 2000, an estimated two and a half million students from eight countries participated,[3] including 150,000 Canadian and 500,000 American students.[4]

❧ Scheduling weekly or monthly Walking Wednesdays to maintain the interest and momentum generated by International Walk to School Day in October. Friendly competitions are often held to entice new walkers to join, with awards given to classes with the highest rates of participation.

Healthier bodies, better air

A motivation behind many walk-to-school programs is rising concern about children's health and fitness. Childhood asthma, a respiratory disease commonly triggered

(continued on page 34)

Organizing a Walking (or Cycling) School Bus

1. INVITE interested members of the school and community to participate in a walkabout survey of school access points and adjacent streets during morning and afternoon pick-up and drop-off times. Identify concerns about safety, traffic, sidewalks, bicycle storage, etc., as well as potential solutions. Invite municipal planners and police to share their expertise in this initial assessment.

2. SEEK SUPPORT in the school and the community. Present the survey findings to school staff and parent councils and establish an organizing committee. Recruit additional partners from the school board, local residents' groups, police, health department and any other community agency that may have resources and expertise to assist you. Ask local businesses to donate printing services for newsletters and announcements, or clothing such as bright scarves or reflective shoelaces which will give visibility to the walking/cycling school bus.

3. CONDUCT PRELIMINARY SURVEYS, asking students and parents about present modes of transport, the reasons for these choices and whether they would consider joining a walking/cycling school bus (see the "Student Survey" on page 42 which may be adapted or extended for this purpose). The responses will help you gauge the interest and concerns of students and parents, and will form a baseline for comparison when evaluating the effectiveness of your program later. Distribute a summary of the survey results to students, teachers and parents.

4. PUBLICIZE the walking school bus in school newsletters and announcements and on posters in the neighborhood. Ask students or parent volunteers to translate materials being sent home into all languages commonly used in your community.

Vélo Québec

5. ESTABLISH BUS ROUTES. In a meeting with interested parents and caregivers, ask participants to put colored pins or stickers on an enlarged map of the school neighborhood to show where they live and how many of their children attend the school. The clusters of pins will help in determining where bus routes are needed, which families will participate in each, and the safest potential routes. Encourage each group of parents to walk these routes before the walking school bus is launched.

6. AGREE ON THE RULES. Each group should establish rules on matters such as waiting for latecomers and notifying drivers of children's absences, along with basic safety rules. Ensure that each "bus driver" has a list of the names and addresses of students and the home and work phone numbers of their parents.

7. MAKE THE BUS VISIBLE by having everyone wear something that is readily identifiable such as reflective shoelaces or zipper pulls on jackets.

8. TAKE A TRIAL WALK with students and parents to establish a pick-up schedule, identify the least safe parts of the route and resolve any unforeseen concerns. Post signs in the neighborhood and school showing the bus routes and after-school meeting places.

9. CELEBRATE WITH AN OFFICIAL LAUNCH and invite local dignitaries and the media to attend. Display students' artwork portraying special sights on their walks to and from school.

10. MAINTAIN SUPPORT by discussing with students the health, environmental and safety benefits of walking and cycling as opposed to driving to school. Include the latest findings on these issues in school newsletters, along with students' stories about their "bus" experiences.

11. EVALUATE YOUR EFFORTS after one year. Survey students and parents again and compare responses with those in the preliminary surveys. Report the results to community partners and develop a strategy for the next year. Seek to have walking/cycling school buses incorporated into school policies and student registration forms.

Source: Go for Green. To obtain more detailed instructions, background information and reproducible surveys, contact Go for Green's Active and Safe Routes to School coordinator at (888) 822-2848, www.goforgreen.ca.

Curriculum links

Language arts: Create bulletins and flyers to inform parents of the program; write stories for the school newsletter about observations and experiences along the walking route; compare and debate the advantages and disadvantages of different modes of transportation.

Art and music: Compose a theme song for a walking school bus; create works of art that portray the people, plants, animals and interesting buildings in the school neighborhood; design colorful badges, sashes or headbands to wear on the walking school bus.

Math: Keep individual and class logs of the distances travelled monthly on foot, by bicycle and by car. Graph the results, calculate percentages, and monitor changes over several months. Calculate the school's reduction in carbon dioxide emissions as a result of the walking program (1 liter of gasoline produces about 2.35 kg of CO_2; 1 U.S. gallon of gasoline produces about 18.8 lbs. of CO_2).

Science and Health: Investigate the impacts of various forms of transportation on human health and the environment; investigate how calorie intake and physical exercise are related to body weight; en route to school, monitor seasonal changes in trees and plants and the migration of birds; observe cloud patterns and practice weather predictions.

Youth Challenge International

Steps in a new direction

- Students at Maurice Cody Public School in Toronto, Ontario, are taking a "virtual walk to the east coast" by plotting their combined walking miles on a map of Canada and learning about the cities and sights along the way.

- One day each week during the fall and spring, school bus drivers bringing children into the small community of St. George, New Brunswick, drop students at a designated spot one kilometer from the school. They are met by parent and teacher volunteers and walk the rest of the way to school along foot trails. Traffic and pollution around the school are reduced considerably, and kids start the day with a healthy dose of exercise and fresh air.

- In Tacoma, Washington, students at Northeast Tacoma Elementary called attention to the lack of sidewalks in their neighborhood by walking along the road carrying signs demanding "Safe Streets for Kids." The resulting media attention spurred the city to install sidewalks.

- In Montréal, Québec, a "Biking School Bus" has eased parents' concerns about children travelling to and from school through the many shaded and secluded areas of a large urban park. Students who cycle to École Le Plateau meet at a designated spot and are led through the park by a parent cyclist.

- The walking school bus "passengers" at John Norquay School in Vancouver have a theme song for their daily walks to and from the school.

- Schools in South Carolina can apply to the Governor's Council of Physical Fitness for mini-grants to initiate walking and cycling programs, a process that encourages schools to develop more ambitious, long-term goals. In California, the Department of Education requires all schools to have a transportation policy that encourages "walk-pools."

For information on organizing walking or cycling school buses, contact: Canada: Active and Safe Routes to School, c/o Go For Green, Ottawa, (888) 822-2848, www.goforgreen.ca. Ontario schools should contact Greenest City at (416) 488-7263, www.greenestcity.org. British Columbia schools should contact Way to Go at (877) 325-3636, www.waytogo.icbc.bc.ca. United States: Walk Our Children to School Day, c/o Harold Thompson, National Safety Council in Itasca, Illinois at (800) 621-7615 x 2383, www.nsc.org/walkable.htm.

by automobile air pollution, has increased four-fold in the past 20 years.[5] And in these days of watching television, playing computer games, and being chauffeured by parents, few children get the exercise they need. In the United States, 35 percent of children watch five hours or more of television each day, and 78 percent fall short of getting the recommended 30 minutes of moderate exercise daily and 20 minutes of vigorous exercise a few times each week.[6] Similarly, the Canadian Fitness and Lifestyle Research Institute reported in 1995 that two-thirds of Canadian children are not active enough to lay a solid foundation for future health and well-being. As many as 20 percent are overweight, and obesity has increased by more than 50 percent in six- to eleven-year-olds in the past 15 years.

Not only does walking help to improve children's physical fitness, it has also been demonstrated that active children tend to perform better academically. Communities, too, are safer and cleaner environments when parents leave their cars at home. For every ten children who join a walking school bus instead of being driven by a parent, there are eight to ten fewer cars creating a traffic hazard and polluting the air in front of the school. In Danish communities where walking programs have been in place for several years, traffic injuries involving children have decreased by as much as 67 percent.[7] After participating for one year in a walking school bus, nine families at a Toronto school calculated that they had prevented about 1,000 kilograms (2,200 pounds) of greenhouse gases from being released into the atmosphere.[8]

As the morning rush-hour traffic grinds slowly along North America's main thoroughfares, parents and children are rediscovering the simple pleasure and freedom of pedestrian travel through the side streets of their neighborhoods. Besides being companionable and fun, walking school buses are a visible reminder of the health, safety and environmental advantages of an old-fashioned and eminently sustainable mode of transportation. ✦

Elise Houghton is a freelance environmental writer in Toronto, Ontario, with a strong interest in public environmental education.

Notes

1   Go for Green, Active and Safe Routes to School coordinator, 2001.
2   U.S. Center for Disease Control and Prevention, Atlanta, Georgia, 2001.
3   National Safety Council, www.nsc.org/walkable.htm, 2001.
4   Go for Green, 2001; Loren Marchetti, Highway Safety Research Center, University of North Carolina, 2001.
5   Go for Green, www.goforgreen.ca, 2001.
6   National Safety Council, www.nsc.org/walkable.htm, 1999.
7   Sustrans' Safe Routes to School (UK), www.sustrans.org.uk, March 1999.
8   Pembina Institute, www.climatechangesolutions.com, 2001.

Building a Community of Life-long Cyclists

by Ken Croxford

When I started bicycling to work year round, the physical and mental benefits were profound. If it works for me, I thought, why not the kids? Cycling promotes fitness, creates no air pollution, and has the potential to play a leading role in reducing greenhouse gas emissions in urban settings. Yet world bicycle production has actually been dropping since 1993, and while in some European cities 20 to 30 percent of trips are made by bike, that figure is closer to one percent in North America.[1]

In our sprawling cities built for cars, many young cyclists are cautioned never to venture beyond their own neighborhoods and most stop riding a bike altogether as they enter the boundary-pushing period of adolescence. Those who do continue riding have the highest accident rate among cyclists, 11- to 14-year-olds accounting for 70 percent of all bike-related injuries. I realized that if I wanted my students to become life-long cyclists, I would need to help them regain their enthusiasm for cycling and become confident and competent in negotiating the roads. Over the course of many years, I have managed to integrate aspects of cycling into many curricular and extra-curricular activities at school, a combination that has been exciting and very rewarding.

As a teacher of Design and Technology, when I learned that approximately half of cycling accidents are due to mechanical problems, I developed a bike mechanics curriculum for shop programs. All students enrolled in my Design and Technology classes are introduced to bike mechanics, and the program has generated tremendous response from students and their families. We collect bikes in any condition from a number of sources: from students' homes, from the curbside on trash day, and from the local police department. Students get hands-on experience as they recondition these formerly loved bikes which are then sent back into the community to their original owners or to less advantaged children. Wherever possible, we add a global dimension to our bicycle program. For a local Bikes Not Bombs project, students reconditioned bikes which were then given to local artists to decorate. The Art Bikes were subsequently auctioned and the money donated to purchase bicycles for teachers and health care workers in developing countries.

As students develop skills, they become quite capable and confident working on their own or their families' bikes. As part of our bike shop service, Bike Check crews are assigned to the elementary schools every spring to do safety checks on all the bikes on site. As many as 300 bikes at four schools are attended to by my grade seven to nine bike shop students. The Bike Check program gives the older kids a chance to develop and use their expertise, and helps the younger kids become more aware of bicycle safety and maintenance.

To encourage year-round and round-the-town bicycle use, I organize a number of weekend activity days for students. Sometimes we pedal 20 kilometers (12 miles) downtown from our suburban neighborhood on a wintry Saturday. At other times, we tour urban parks

Photographs by Ken Croxford

Top: A student bike shop crew keeps the wheels turning and teaches younger students about cycling safety. Bottom: Students gather for a winter bike outing with their teacher.

to learn safe and environmentally responsible off-road cycling habits. With the help of other cyclists I developed a ten-hour extra-curricular cycling course for young people called Cycle Right which is now part of the Can Bike programs across Canada, and similar to the Effective Cycling programs in the United States.

As students learn how to ride safely on city streets, how to dress appropriately for the weather, and how to maintain and repair their bikes, they begin to appreciate the feasibility of using bicycles as a regular, all-season mode of transportation. This, after all, has been the hidden agenda in my efforts to encourage interest in cycling. The bicycle is a simple machine, user-friendly and remarkably durable and practical. Its significance as a part of the transportation network reaches far beyond our schoolyards and neighborhoods. Over the years, there have been many opportunities to open eyes and minds to an appreciation

The bicycle's significance as a part of the transportation network reaches far beyond our schoolyards and neighborhoods.

of how practical a solution the bicycle is to many environmental and transportation problems. At the core of our efforts have been the three Rs: we can reduce the use of cars by encouraging cycling; we can reuse unwanted bikes by reconditioning them and getting them back into circulation; and we can recycle bicycle parts for bike repairs and other uses. The spinoffs of the program have been greater numbers of students cycling to school year-round, increased use of helmets, fewer accidents, higher levels of environmental awareness and physical fitness — and many more students signing up to get their hands dirty working on the original Green Machine. ❧

Ken Croxford is an environmental educator and cycling advocate in Toronto, Ontario.

Note
1   Lester R. Brown, Michael Renner and Brian Halweil, Worldwatch Institute, *Vital Signs 1999* (New York: Norton and Co., 1999), p. 84.

Put bicycling into your school's Green Plan

Classroom activities
- Create a bike center in your classroom with magazines, articles, posters, pictures and brochures related to bicycles and cycling.
- Bring in a bike and label the parts. Use a bicycle to demonstrate principles of mechanics and motion and the design and function of wheels, levers and gears.
- Devise a means of generating electricity using bicycle power.
- Explore various aspects of cycling such as racing competitions and the use of bicycles around the world.
- Trace the history of bicycles and improvements in their design and materials over time.
- Examine the financial, environmental and social costs and benefits of cycling compared with other forms of transportation.

School and extra-curricular activities
- Start a school bike club.
- Create posters or newsletters and organize assemblies to encourage students and staff to ride their bikes to school.
- Be an advocate for bike-friendly schools (ensure secure parking, safe routes and easy access).
- Offer extra-curricular cycling activities (instructor certification is strongly recommended for this).
- Start a bike recycling and parts exchange program, and hold a bike exchange in the spring.
- Contact police and bike shops for discarded bikes that can be reconditioned and sold to raise funds for club projects.

- Decorate bikes and hold a bicycle art auction.
- Start a bicycle polo team.
- Train a bike check crew.
- Work with parent and community groups to promote the use of helmets.

Become a certified cycling instructor
Contact your provincial or state cycling association and inquire about programs such as Can Bike in Canada or Effective Cycling in the United States. In addition to instructor training, these programs offer "driver ed" bike courses for grades six to eight, and adult courses that combine classroom instruction with on-road handling skills.

It Takes a Whole Bus to Educate a Child: A Reading

by Arthur Orsini

There are many things we cannot teach our children. They need to be around and learn from strangers. It's one of those it-takes-a-village-to-raise-child kind of things. And so I am glad we rely on the bus. It's very educational. Public transit is relatively cheap and my kids love it because they get to meet and talk with a variety of people. Well, okay, not the very rich, but pretty much everyone else. I can't think of any other public space where they have such liberty with strangers and I have no anxiety about it. They talk to anyone: seniors, radicals, sleepyheads, lovers, business people and teenagers.

Earlier on in their lives they had trouble understanding that everyone had different destinations. With wide eyes they would ask, "Are you going to visit Aunt Elaina, too?" Imagine the wonder in learning that she is going shopping, he's off to work and another is coming home from work. And here we are, together, on the same bus! It's natural for a child to become animated around such wonders, but I have been constantly surprised at how people perk up in response. Certainly it is the silver-haired women who are most attentive, but older men are a surprise second. These are the five- or ten-minute grandparents of varying race and culture who have all the time in the world to chat. Talking seems to keep my kids from staring. Staring, after all, is just a wasted opportunity when your mind is full of questions. They talk to everyone, having learned that, on a bus, I am not likely to answer their questions about fellow passengers. Ask them yourself, I say. Start with hello, be respectful, and listen for the answer before you ask another. So they do. And by and large they have a captive audience.

"Why do you sit in a wheelchair?"
"Why is your hair green?"
"What is that bead doing in your nose?"
"What's on your head?"
"Why don't you have a baby?"

I listen to everything, ready to intercept or make amends. Yet despite their skill at infuriating each other, they have never been rude to strangers on the bus. We've met university students who went through great pains to explain their course of study in simple English. Drunken men have made funny faces to get them laughing out loud. The kids have touched pink hair, something they've never had the opportunity to do at home. They once barked and meowed in chorus with a bus driver for 15 blocks on the 99 Express, and to their great delight were greeted with a meow on the bus home. "It's the same driver! It's the same driver!" my daughter screamed. Meow, woof, all the way back again.

Some people seem to need only a small nudge to break from the stoic commuter shell. We've met irritable people: impatient to retrieve their car from the mechanic, huffy at having even to be on the bus. Young guys, early twenties, out to impress a couple of preschoolers, say, "Once I get my car back, I won't be taking the bus again." My kids are shocked. "Cars do big damage," my daughter will say. And somehow I believe she is recalling the balloon that got run down on West 12th back in '96.

My son claimed to have learned to read at age three: whenever the bell rang, he'd point to the front of the bus, slide his finger from left to right and proudly read "NEXT STOP!" My daughter, despite our bidding, prefers to stand and is the first to get up and offer her seat to anyone older. They know that the #15 becomes a #17 when it gets downtown. They know that the #100 goes to the airport and they beg us to take a trip so we can board that bus.

I have learned, too. I used to hush their questions to strangers until it became clear how unoffensive it was and how much they got out of it. But I hadn't even noticed what public transit was doing to my children until an elderly woman, getting out at our stop, grabbed hold of my elbow. She told me how charmed and impressed she was by my then three-year-old daughter's conversation skills. Without thinking, I replied, "It's because we don't have a car. We take the bus a lot." It takes a busload to raise a child. ✎

Arthur Orsini is a writer and School Trip-Reduction Coordinator of the Better Environmentally Sound Transportation in Vancouver, British Columbia.

57

Investigating Public Transit

by Tim Grant, Gail Littlejohn and Arthur Orsini

The following activities use the reading "It Takes a Whole Bus to Educate a Child" (page 37) as a starting point in exploring the social, economic and environmental issues associated with the use of public transit.

Grades K-3

Bus Basics: Discuss with your class: What is a bus? Who has ridden on a bus? What places have you gone? Discuss why people use buses.

Investigate: How much is the bus fare in your community? How do you find a bus stop? What bus route is closest to the school? Why does the bus change its name when it reaches its destination? What is a transfer and how do you read it? If you are lost or feel you are in danger, how can a bus driver help you?

Bus Field Trip:
Take the students on a bus ride. Recruiting parents to assist will allow you to divide the class into manageable groups. Your local transit authority can advise on the best time of day to travel with young students, and may be able to send a representative to answer questions about the transit system. Students may follow up by drawing pictures or writing poems or stories about their public-transit excursion.

Grades 4-6

Mapping Routes: In addition to the investigations for grades K-3, students can gather the following facts: How early and late do the buses run in your community? How can riders find out the schedule for a bus route (e.g., published schedules, postings at bus stops, help lines, websites)? Obtain route maps and schedules from

Photographs by Toronto Transit Commission

How much of our public space is given to cars? Students demonstrate the road-saving advantages of public transit in downtown Toronto.

your transit company and challenge students to map out the most direct routes between various points.

Transit Pros and Cons: The author of "It Takes a Whole Bus..." suggests several benefits of taking public transit. What are they? What other advantages can you think of? What disadvantages are there? Chart these pros and cons under headings such as social, economic and environmental.

Transit Survey: Conduct a survey of transit use by taking a poll of parents and neighbors. How many ride public transit? How often? For what types of trips is public transit most suitable? If some people do not use transit, what are the reasons? How could bus service be made more attractive? Collect the responses, develop a report that includes recommendations, and send it to your city councillor and transit authority.

Grades 7-9

The following activities require students to obtain information from the local transit authority, roads department and other public agencies.

Cars and Air Quality: When burned in an internal combustion engine, one liter of gasoline produces 2.35 kilograms of carbon dioxide (18.8 lbs/US gallon), while one liter of diesel fuel produces 2.77 kilograms (22.1 lbs/US gallon). Estimate how much carbon dioxide is emitted by transit vehicles and by private vehicles in your community. What other air pollutants (e.g., SO_2, NOx, ozone), and how much, are produced by transit and private vehicles? At what time of the day, the week and the year is air pollution at its highest and lowest in your community? What accounts for these differences? Develop a transportation plan that would help to reduce air pollution by reducing the number of vehicles on the road.

Transportation

Promoting Public Transit: Obtain copies of marketing and advertising materials from your local transit company. Discuss the messages they communicate, the intended audience, and the advertising techniques used. How effective are the ads in convincing people to use public transit? Have students create an advertising campaign to urge other students to ride public transit; this could include posters placed in hallways and a skit performed at a school assembly.

Grades 10-12

The following activities require students to obtain information from the local transit authority, roads department and other public agencies.

Who Pays?

Direct costs: In most communities the money for building and maintaining roads comes from general tax revenues. Estimate the average local road expenditure per vehicle and per passenger in public transit vehicles and private vehicles. Students will need to gather the following information: a) the annual budget for building and maintaining roads in your community; b) the average number of private vehicles and transit vehicles on the road on a typical weekday; c) the average number of people riding in each private vehicle and transit vehicle.

Indirect costs: Brainstorm some of the indirect costs of local transportation such as policing and accident-related expenditures. Contact the local police department, ambulance services and health care agencies to obtain rough estimates of: a) the time/cost of policing public transit (monitoring vehicles and facilities) versus the time/cost of policing private cars and trucks (directing traffic, ticketing, investigating accidents); b) the cost of providing ambulance service to accidents involving transit vehicles versus accidents involving private vehicles; and c) the number of passenger injuries and related health care costs in transit vehicles versus in private cars.

Develop a chart comparing the direct and indirect costs of public and private transportation. Discuss your findings. Do people who drive cars pay their fair share of direct and indirect costs? If not, what could be done to

distribute costs more equitably? How do car drivers benefit from having a public transit system (e.g., reduced road congestion, the convenience of having the option to take public transit)? Should car drivers pay an extra levy to support public transit?

Community Planning: Referring to a map of your community, discuss the reasons that people commute long distances (e.g., suburban sprawl, zoning bylaws that prevent mixing business and residential uses, deterioration of inner-city housing, a concentration of workplaces such as industrial parks on the edge of town). Redesign the community in a way that would allow people to travel shorter distances, ideally without their cars, to work and shop.

Healthy Communities: In "It Takes a Whole Bus...", riding the bus gives the children opportunities to encounter and appreciate human diversity. Similarly, adults seem to benefit from the opportunity to talk to the kids. To what extent do people talk to strangers in your community? Where is this most likely to occur? Discuss the importance of this social interaction in building healthy communities.

Alternatives to Buses: Until the 1940s, electric railways or streetcars were the main form of public transit in North American cities. Some cities are now bringing them back. Research the history of electric railways and explain the reasons for their decline. Compare the relative advantages and disadvantages of buses and streetcars.

Comparing Fuels: Most North American buses are powered by diesel fuel, which emits high levels of carbon dioxide, nitrous oxides and other particulates. Compare the costs and benefits of other fuel sources such as natural gas and fuel cells. ❦

Tim Grant and Gail Littlejohn are editors of Green Teacher *magazine in Toronto, Ontario. Arthur Orsini is a writer and School Trip-Reduction Coordinator of the Better Environmentally Sound Transportation in Vancouver, British Columbia.*

Going Off-Ramp: A Car Trip Reduction Plan for Schools

by Arthur Orsini

 Morning traffic congestion at schools has become the norm all across North America. Here in Vancouver, a 1995 study showed that the number of students arriving by car had increased by 53 percent within a decade. This trend is a threat both to our air quality and to our students' health and fitness. It also poses a safety risk for those who choose to walk or cycle to school.

Over time, we have let our definition of the driving distance to school get shorter and shorter. Yet it is these short, routine, local trips to school that present the best opportunity to counter the car-driving trend. Organizing a car trip reduction program in your school can raise awareness of the health, financial and environmental benefits of more sustainable transportation choices such as walking, cycling, skating, car pooling and using public transit. It can also overcome many of the perceived barriers to these modes of transportation.

Working with student leaders in nine urban and suburban communities in the Vancouver and Victoria regions, Better Environmentally Sound Transportation is piloting an out-of-class initiative to reduce car trips to secondary schools. The primary goal of the *off ramp* program is to reduce the average number of cars coming daily to these schools by at least 20 percent. To achieve this goal, we have developed three broad objectives that could be used by any school group to reduce car use among students and staff. The first is to raise awareness of transportation issues and related environmental effects. The second is to organize school-wide events such as Cycle-to-School Days or Car-free Days that encourage students and staff to try alternatives to the car. Building on this crack in the everyone-drives-a-car attitude, the third objective is to strengthen the sustainable transportation infrastructure within the school community. Ranging from posting bus routes and schedules to installing bike shelters, the focus is on making it easier for students to use the alternatives.

Any school group can use the *off ramp* framework to develop car trip reduction strategies suited to their community. The following are guidelines for planning and implementing a successful program.

Expect Long Delays: Vancouver students prepare a window display dramatizing the problem of traffic congestion.

Planning

It is important to gauge at the outset how much time your group will be able to commit to the program during the school year. This will determine just how realistic is the planned sequence of events. While a car trip reduction program could be of any duration, most groups will need a minimum of three months for planning, implementation and evaluation. It is also helpful to brainstorm how many of the components of the program could be handled as classroom assignments; for example, classroom activities might include tallying surveys, making posters, planning events and publicity, and writing letters. At the same time, brainstorm which local stores might donate prizes that can be given to students who switch to more sustainable means of transportation.

Surveys conducted at the beginning, middle and end of the program are vital for planning and evaluating a campaign. To assess current transportation habits and to uncover barriers to using sustainable transportation options, we have developed three different surveys. An initial school-wide survey to find out how each student and teacher got to school that day gives a snapshot of current practices. This quick, hands-up classroom poll may be used several times: to get a baseline measurement before the program is announced to the school, to assess progress following awareness-raising events, and to evaluate the longer term results weeks after those events have ended.

Just after the first hands-up school-wide survey is conducted, an extended survey in the form of a questionnaire is given to 10 to 15 percent of the students. This questionnaire (see page 42) asks why students choose to travel the way they do and what would encourage them to walk, cycle, take public transit or join a car pool. At the same time, a third survey is prepared, in as many of the school's languages as possible, that asks parents and caregivers who pick up and drop off students to identify any concerns they have about their teenaged children switching to other modes of transportation. This last survey also helps to publicize the car trip reduction program throughout the community.

A transportation game challenges contestants at a Youth Week rally.

The survey responses help define the themes used to promote sustainable transportation. For example, at University Hill Secondary School in Vancouver, the first school-wide survey revealed the following split: 38 percent walked, 28 percent took public transit, 17 percent travelled alone by car, 15 percent car-pooled and only 2 percent cycled. With this information, the school's Environmental Club decided to focus their efforts on cycling. Thus they paid close attention to responses to the questions in the extended student survey that dealt with cycling. When asked "Why do you cycle to school?" the most frequent comment was "It's fast and I can make my own schedule." This led the group to create posters highlighting the independence that cycling offers young people. They featured slogans such as "Cyclists don't need to ask their parents for bus fare," "Cyclists don't wait for their parents in the morning," "Cyclists don't ask to use the car... until the weekend." Finally, as a first step in addressing the most frequently mentioned barrier to cycling — the lack of secure, sheltered bike racks at the school — another series of posters described how to lock a bicycle securely and where to find inexpensive "jalopy" bikes that are less likely to be stolen.

Whichever sustainable transportation option becomes the focus of your car trip reduction program, it is important to remember that encouraging people to drive less requires diplomacy.

Implementation

Your group may wish to align the start of the program with an event such as Earth Day, Clean Air Day, Environment Week or the spring or fall equinox. Whenever you start, consider using promotional tools such as posters, bike rallies (mass rides), bike maintenance workshops, sign-ups for car pool and walking buddies, transit displays near school exits showing routes and schedules, and prizes such as water bottles, stickers, buttons, tee-shirts and edible treats. These prizes and promotions will generate enthusiasm and help to convince students that the alternatives to driving are both practical and realistic. Even a short-term surge in bike riding, such as on a designated Cycle-to-School Day, will demonstrate how many students actually do own bikes and portray cycling as a normal activity. Depending on the support from other teachers in the school, transportation issues could also be addressed in a number of subjects through topics such as health, fitness, land use, gasoline prices, traffic safety, air quality and climate change.

Once tabulated, the school-wide and extended survey results will indicate which form of sustainable transportation looks to be the easiest switch from car travel for your community. Promoting this transportation option will become the focus of the program. If, for instance, the goal is to increase the number of cycling commuters, attention would focus on enhancing cycling skills, providing repair workshops, mapping safe cycling routes, and securing places to lock up bikes. All of these measures will increase the profile of and commitment to cycling, boost confidence, and help to eliminate the perceived barriers to its usage.

Evaluation

The final round of surveys reveals to what extent transportation choices have changed as a result of the program and whether there is greater awareness of the effect of these choices on air quality and atmospheric concentrations of greenhouse gases. This sets the stage for the last phase of the program. Consider publicizing your results in the wider community, including giving an estimate of the carbon dioxide emissions that were avoided as a result of the program. Having uncovered various barriers to more sustainable forms of transportation, consider writing letters to the municipal government requesting the installation of such amenities as additional sidewalks, crosswalks and bicycle lanes. Ask the school district to install sheltered bike racks if they are needed. Write to the local transit authority requesting bus shelters, route improvements, and schedules that coincide with the beginning and end of the school day.

Whichever sustainable transportation option becomes the focus of your car trip reduction program, it is important to remember that encouraging people to drive less requires diplomacy. Most drivers are already aware of the pollution caused by automobiles. And it is not always attitudinal barriers that keep people from using other forms of transportation; they may also have encountered physical barriers such as infrequent bus service, lack of sidewalks, or regional roads perceived as unsafe for cycling or walking. Nevertheless, you are likely to hear from colleagues and students all kinds of reasons why

they must use their cars and why the alternatives available to them are insufficient or impractical. You might want to challenge them to begin reducing their car use by eliminating one trip per week, reminding them that you are not asking them to get rid of their cars completely. It is worthwhile to remember that the car itself is not the problem we wish to address. The long-term goal is to reduce car traffic in and around the school, to encourage people to become life-long walkers, cyclists and transit-users, and to create an aware — and physically healthy — population who think twice about getting into a car for a short trip. §

Arthur Orsini is the off ramp *coordinator at Better Environmentally Sound Transportation (B.E.S.T.) in Vancouver, British Columbia. In 2000, the international Organization for Economic Co-operation and Development selected the* off ramp *program for one of its Best Practices in Environmentally Sustainable Transport awards.*

For further information or to obtain copies of the other off ramp *surveys, call B.E.S.T. at (604) 669-2860 or visit www.best.bc.ca.*

Student Survey

off ramp

Please complete this survey about getting to school. In one of your classes, you've already been asked **HOW** you got to school, but this time we need to hear a bit about **WHY** you travel to school the way(s) that you do.

We will hold a draw on _____ at _____. Be sure you've completed and handed this in so it can be entered in the draw for prizes.

name _____ grade _____

homeroom _____

Please answer ALL of the following questions.

1. How do you usually get to school?
❑ walking   ❑ cycling   ❑ taking transit   ❑ by car with another student
❑ by car on your own (*if you are the only student in your car, this is the one to check*)

Do you think this is an environmentally friendly way of getting school? Why or why not? _____
_____

2. Why do you walk to school? (check as many as apply)
❑ It wakes me up   ❑ I never walk   ❑ It's good exercise
❑ I never walk when it's cold/raining   ❑ I can walk with a friend   ❑ It's free
❑ I like the route I take
❑ other _____

3. Why do you cycle to school? (check as many as apply)
❑ It wakes me up   ❑ I never cycle   ❑ It's good exercise
❑ I never cycle when it's cold/raining   ❑ It's fast and I make my own schedule
❑ It's inexpensive   ❑ I like the route I take
❑ other _____

continued on next page ➤

4. Why do you take public transit to school? (check as many as apply)

❏ I get time to talk with my friends on the way ❏ I don't have to rely on my parents
❏ It's inexpensive ❏ There's a bus stop near my home and the school
❏ I have a schedule and the bus is usually on time ❏ I never take the bus
❏ I never take the bus when it's cold/raining
❏ other _____

5. Why do you drive (or get driven) to school? (check as many as apply)

❏ It's fast ❏ I can always find free parking
❏ Someone picks me up ❏ It keeps out of the rain/cold weather
❏ It's free (someone else is paying for car and gas)
❏ There are other places that I have to get to on the way (i.e., work)
❏ I never go by car ❏ I drive only when it's cold/raining
❏ other _____

6. What would encourage you to walk to school? (check as many as apply)

❏ finding someone to walk with ❏ making the roads and crosswalks safer near the school
❏ fewer cars in and around the school grounds
❏ other _____

7. What would encourage you to cycle to school? (check as many as apply)

❏ offer bicycle 'clinics' for safety and maintenance ❏ secure, sheltered racks to lock my bike
❏ safer cycling routes to school ❏ a place to hang wet rain gear (other than my locker)
❏ other _____

8. What would encourage you to take the bus to school? (check as many as apply)

❏ rain shelters at the bus stop ❏ more frequent buses
❏ bus stops closer to school ❏ bus stops closer to home
❏ posting bus schedules and route information near the school exits
❏ other

9. How could we reduce the number of cars coming to school? (check as many as apply)

❏ encourage drivers to pick up other students on the way
❏ set up a carpool system to connect cars with students living nearby
❏ start charging for student parking/raise the parking fees
❏ other _____

10. If you were to take an alternative form of transportation instead of driving to school, which would it most likely be? (check only one)

❏ walking ❏ cycling ❏ taking transit ❏ joining a carpool

because _____

_____

thanks

From Gridlock to Global Warming

*A high school unit investigating the link between
local transportation issues and global climate change*

by Rebecca Watts Hull

Most environmental educators would agree that encouraging students to "think globally" is important. At the same time, teachers recognize that global issues can seem overwhelming to young people, and that local problems are often more engaging and more easily investigated first-hand. How do we help students to think globally while also keeping environmental investigation local and relevant? One way is to investigate a local issue that is connected to a global problem. The following four-week unit aims to do just that. Developed for a high school environmental science class in Atlanta, Georgia, the unit focuses on problems associated with urban transportation. After exploring local issues in depth, students look at the links between the transportation dilemma and the worldwide concern about global warming.

Community Bicycle Network, Toronto

Selecting the topic

I selected transportation as the theme of the unit because Atlanta, like many other North American cities, is facing serious problems of traffic congestion and poor air quality linked to heavy car use. Atlantans now have the longest (with respect to time) average commute of anyone in the world. Commuters are frustrated by gridlock, and yet many who could travel by train or bus still choose to drive; and Metro Atlanta counties without adequate public transportation continue to vote down initiatives to extend rail lines to their communities. As a result of all the single-passenger driving, Atlanta's air quality is so bad that it threatens health. Local media periodically highlight these issues, and several local groups have organized to address the problem.

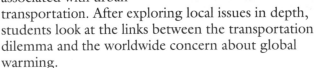

The students who participated in this unit were, or soon would be, licensed drivers, and all had experienced local traffic congestion first-hand. Media coverage had also helped to underscore its relevance to them. We began the unit at a time when Atlanta had just been denied federal funds for road construction because the city's poor air quality had it in violation of the Clean Air Act. At the same time, world leaders had just met in Kyoto to draft a treaty to address the problem of global warming. The timeliness of these issues, both locally and globally, meant that students had heard something about them and had ready access to newspaper articles and Internet sites addressing them.

To introduce the unit, I asked students to read background information on the impact of road travel and opportunities for alternatives in the Atlanta area. We discussed a variety of points of view on the city's traffic congestion and its environmental impacts. The students had learned about the use of non-renewable resources in a previous unit and therefore already knew some of the impacts of the heavy use of fossil fuels. Once they had a general familiarity with local transportation issues, I introduced the unit's driving question: "What are the impacts of daily transportation decisions in Metro Atlanta?"

While I selected the overall question for the unit, the class as a group brainstormed specific sub-questions that we would research in order to answer it (see sidebar). We organized these sub-questions into four categories: Current Transportation Patterns, Transportation Alternatives, Health and Environmental Impacts, and Who Makes the Decisions? Students formed four committees, one for each category, to research the sub-questions, and roles were assigned and timelines developed within each working group.

Gathering and sharing information

In order to answer their assigned questions, students searched the Internet, used periodical databases to locate articles, and contacted local politicians and organizations. The sub-question committees organized the information gathered and assigned responsibilities for presenting it both orally and in writing. Each student group gave short presentations to the class on their assigned questions, and we then identified gaps in information and assigned additional research.

In class discussions and journal entries, students indicated intended behavior changes such as considering fuel efficiency when purchasing a vehicle, and trying to walk or bicycle more often in their neighborhoods.

While working on filling in these gaps, we read and discussed articles highlighting success stories from other cities that had faced the same problems of rapid growth and deteriorating environmental quality that Atlanta currently faces — most notably Portland, Oregon, and Chattanooga, Tennessee. While few cities have solved these problems completely, we looked at the positive steps they have taken, and students discussed in groups and wrote in their journals about which steps would be most effective in Atlanta, and why. Many students had displayed a defeatist attitude about the problem we were studying ("It's really bad, but there's nothing to be done about it"), and learning of other communities' successful efforts to solve similar traffic problems helped them move beyond this attitude. With these examples to get us started, together with solutions proposed by Atlanta decision-makers, we developed a list of solutions to the problems caused by excessive automobile traffic.

Town council role-play

The final section of our study of the local situation was a role-play of a town meeting convened to discuss alternatives for the use of federal transportation dollars. We identified key stakeholders — real people we thought would be invited to attend such a meeting — by noting the individuals and organizations that were consulted and quoted in local newspaper articles on the transportation issue. These stakeholders included local politicians, government agency representatives, and citizen group leaders. Students were assigned a character and were required to thoroughly research that person's position on the issue.

Because students' comfort and skill levels with role-play varied greatly, I invited a professional actress who is a consultant to our school to lead a mini-workshop on role-playing. She gave the students tips on researching their character, getting into the role and rehearsing the role. The guidelines she provided helped the students develop questions to ask of the real people they would portray, and helped them identify the traits that might affect their characters' behavior during a town hall meeting like the one we would simulate.

Students followed the guidelines presented in the role-play workshop to develop a "character profile" which included the person's environment, temperament, values and goals. Based on background information and actual statements made by the people they were portraying, each student then developed a half-page position statement indicating how the participant proposed transportation funds to be spent, and why. Copies of these statements were distributed to each student so they could prepare rebuttals to positions that differed greatly from their own. The final task was to prepare index cards with their opening statement and rebuttals to opposing positions.

Unit Question:
"What are the impacts of daily transportation decisions?

Subcategory 1: Current Transportation Patterns
- How many drivers are on the road?
- What public transit options do we currently have?
- What are the comparative costs of different transportation options? (for the individual)
- How do roadbuilding and maintenance costs compare with rail and bus system costs? (for the city/taxpayer)

Subcategory 2: Transportation Alternatives
- What changes in public transportation are currently in the planning stages?
- How are other cities of a similar size dealing with their transportation needs and concerns?
- What does the public think about expanding public transportation? (pro and con)
- What requirements have to be met before Atlanta can once again receive federal transportation funds?

Subcategory 3: Health and Environmental Impacts
- How many road accidents do we have? Deaths and injuries?
- What are the human health impacts of auto emissions?
- What are the environmental impacts of auto emissions?
- What are the environmental impacts of road expansion?

Subcategory 4: Who Makes the Decisions, and How?
- What does the regional commission (or similar body) do?
- How is the federal, state or provincial government involved in municipal transportation decisions?
- Which elected officials are responsible for making decisions about public transit and road construction?
- What nongovernmental groups are involved in transportation issues?

When students had fully prepared for their roles, we conducted a dress rehearsal. The rehearsal allowed me to identify strengths and weaknesses in performances and offer tips and specific guidelines as needed. (Students had particular difficulty remembering to behave as their character would behave rather than as they would.) We then conducted and videotaped the role-play. Students dressed as their characters: for example, the mayor of Atlanta wore a three-piece suit, whereas the president of a local bicycling advocacy group wore a warm-up suit and bike helmet. We later reviewed the videotape and discussed what went well and what aspects could be improved upon next time. Each student critiqued his or her own performance as well as that of one other student.

Linking the local issue to global warming

Once the students had thoroughly investigated and examined the local issues surrounding heavy automobile use, culminating with the role-play exercise, we began to discuss the connection between these local issues and the worldwide issue of global warming. The direct connection between vehicle emissions and the greenhouse effect facilitated this link, and was made even more relevant by the timing of the unit approximately one month following the international meeting on climate change in Kyoto.

I introduced this section of the unit with a lecture on the greenhouse effect and global warming. We then referred back to data collected earlier on the environmental impacts of automobile use to establish the link between the local problem we had been studying and this global concern. We used up-to-date information from the Internet and recent newspaper articles to investigate the major positions presented at the global warming conference in Kyoto. We discussed the U.S. government's position and compared it with that of most European countries and with developing nations, always trying to bear in mind its relationship to Atlanta's air quality problems. The U.S. government proposed cuts in carbon dioxide emissions that would be less drastic than those proposed by other industrialized nations, and pushed for participation by developing nations who wanted to see the industrialized West take the first steps. We discussed possible motives for the U.S. position, and made connections between this position and some of the arguments made regarding Atlanta's air quality problem.

I presented the current status of the Kyoto treaty, and explained ratification and the steps that would be taken in the U.S. to decide whether or not to ratify the treaty. We read and discussed several newspaper and Internet articles describing positions for and against ratification, and students began to develop their own opinions on the issue. Students then found out who their congressional representatives were (using the House website www.house.gov), and began drafting letters arguing for or against ratification. These letters were mailed and all the students received

responses from the representatives that outlined their point of view on the issue. It was exciting for students to realize that their letters to Congress could actually influence whether or not the United States would ratify the treaty.

Evaluation

Student Assessment: Students' work was evaluated half on individual performance and half on group performance in the following:

- Written and oral responses of the working groups to sub-questions.

- Students' written position statements and their performances during the mock town council meeting.

- Self- and peer-evaluations of the role-play.

The skyline of Atlanta: air quality so poor that the city has been in violation of the Clean Air Act.

Joe and Monica Cook

Unit Objectives

Content outcomes: Students will be able to:

- describe the role of vehicle emissions in air pollution, including specific links to acid rain and the greenhouse effect;
- explain the impact of choosing more versus less fuel efficient vehicles;
- describe and diagram the process of global warming and its possible impacts on the Earth;
- describe at least five different perspectives/points of views on local transportation decisions and explain the reasoning behind each;
- describe at least three significant alternatives to private vehicle use and discuss the advantages and disadvantage of each;
- explain the reasoning behind transportation decisions made by friends and neighbors;
- explain their government's position on the Kyoto Protocol treaty on climate change;
- describe their personal opinions on local mass transit opportunities and on the Kyoto Protocol treaty.

Skill outcomes: Students will be able to:

- identify their local, state and national political representatives;
- effectively research and role play the part of a stakeholder in an environmental controversy;
- use the Internet and library periodical databases to collect information on local environmental issues;
- write a clear and concise letter to their local and national representatives explaining their position on a pending decision.

- Letters to congressional representatives on the position of the U.S. government on the Kyoto global warming treaty.
- Written reflections on the issues and unit in journals.

Unit Evaluation: The students evaluated the unit in two ways: through group discussion in class, and privately in a journal entry. I found that the combination of these two techniques was very effective in soliciting honest feedback about the style and content of the unit. The group discussion was structured around three questions: what went well? what did not go well? and what would we do differently next time?

In addition, I conducted a brief pre-test/post-test to measure, albeit very roughly, change in students' knowledge and attitudes as a result of the unit. This assessment was not graded. Students were asked to respond as completely and with as much detail as they could to the unit's driving question: "What are the impacts of daily transportation decisions in Metro Atlanta?" The pre-test was conducted immediately before beginning the unit; the post-test was given immediately after concluding it. This comparison gave a qualitative measure of the difference in students' understanding as a result of the unit. For most students, it revealed a more complex understanding of the different points of view and alternatives for dealing with the problem.

While the pre-test/post-test measurement did show changes in knowledge and understanding, it is important to note that such assessments do not measure behavioral change, considered by many to be the ultimate goal of environmental education. In class discussions and journal entries, students indicated intended behavior changes such as considering fuel efficiency when purchasing a vehicle, and trying to walk or bicycle more often in their neighborhoods. It is very difficult, however, to predict the impact of such learning on adult behavior.

Notes on teaching strategies

Student-centered Investigation: This unit followed a student-centered project-based approach that can be modified to fit the readiness of the students for independent investigation. The students had some experience with independent investigation but their comfort levels with this approach varied highly. As a

Community Bicycle Network, Toronto

Many students had displayed a defeatist attitude about the problem we were studying. Learning of other communities' successful efforts to solve similar traffic problems helped them move beyond this attitude.

result, I designed the original driving question myself and took a central role in guiding the students through the selection of sub-questions and the development of work group tasks. Later in the year, we followed a similar approach to investigate the controversy surrounding logging in the habitat of the spotted owl. This time I had the students themselves select the driving question and gave them a much larger role in defining the process by which they would investigate the issue.

I suggest carefully assessing your students' experience and comfort level with independent investigation, as well as their research skills, before deciding how much of the curriculum design for this unit to take on yourself and how much to leave to students. The project-based approach requires a great deal of initiative and independent research, which is exciting to some students but can be tremendously intimidating to those more accustomed to teacher-centered approaches. In addition, there may be a great deal of variation in students' research skills. Unless your students have followed this approach in previous years, I would not suggest trying it at the beginning of the school year. I have found that slowly easing students into roles of increasing responsibility increases the likelihood of their eventually participating successfully in a project-based unit. Begin with short individual and group research assignments early in the year, slowly increasing the extent to which the students are expected to shape the investigations themselves.

Research Strategies and Information Sources: The research for this unit relied heavily on newspaper articles and "cold calls" to area groups and politicians. To facilitate involvement in the compilation of newspaper articles, have students clip one environment-related article from the local paper each week from the first week of school onward. This ensures that plenty of relevant articles will be on hand when needed, and serves the additional function of getting students in the habit of using local news sources.

Making cold calls was the most challenging aspect of the role-play assignment for most students. They were very nervous about calling people they did not know, and tended to give up very easily when given the run-around. I modelled appropriate phone etiquette for them in the classroom, and even had them practice, but these approaches did not help everyone overcome their nervousness. I later discovered that what had worked best was making a phone call myself with students present. I suggest choosing one of the more difficult calls to be made, perhaps to a busy politician, and having all of the students gather around while you make the call.

All the information used in the unit was gathered by me (e.g., newspaper clippings) or by students, with the exception of basic information on the greenhouse effect and global warming which is available in most environmental science textbooks. It is important to accept that you will be learning along with the students when you follow a project-based approach, and not to worry when they ask questions that you cannot answer. You will, however, need to be prepared to guide them to useful sources that can provide answers. (See suggestions in sidebar below.)

After studying local transportation, students stencilled drains to call attention to the environmental impact of runoff from roads and the dumping of pollutants into storm drains.

Although this unit focused on traffic and air quality in Atlanta, it could be easily adapted for use in almost any urban area, as most cities in North America are facing, or soon will face, the crisis that Atlanta is experiencing. Regardless of where you live, investigating transportation issues locally is one way to help your students begin to think globally about the worldwide problem of climate change, and to better understand the issues and international negotiations surrounding it. Just as important, starting with the local makes the global problem less overwhelming and helps students identify the steps that they themselves can take to have an impact. ⚛

Rebecca Watts Hull is the Science and Math Curriculum Consultant at The Howard School in Atlanta, Georgia.

Reference:
Gardner, Howard. *Frames of Mind: The Theory of Multiple Intelligences.* New York: Basic Books, 1983.

Using Multiple Intelligences: This unit was designed with Howard Gardner's multiple intelligences in mind. Students tend to be more easily motivated when projects allow them to use their areas of strength, or "intelligences." As these vary a great deal among students, incorporating as many as possible into the design and evaluation of curricula ensures that each student has an opportunity to work in his or her area of strength. A summary of how various intelligences were incorporated into the curriculum design is given below.

Bodily-Kinesthetic: Preparation and performance of character's personality in the role-play.

Spatial: Analysis of existing and proposed land-use and mass transit maps for Metro Atlanta.

Linguistic: Written position statement, and opening statement and oral arguments during role-play; persuasive letter on global warming to representative.

Interpersonal: Interaction with other characters during role-play; teamwork on project research; character research (phone calls and other direct contact).

Intrapersonal: Preparation for character role; reflection on personal attitudes and opinions through journal entries.

Logical-Mathematical: Preparation of rebuttals for role-play; analysis and evaluation of evidence for global warming; argument for or against treaty based on evidence.

Transportation and Global Warming Resources

Greenhouse effect/Global warming:
- Textbooks and Internet
- EPA regional office (videos, curricula)
- Major environmental organizations such as World Resources Institute, World Wildlife Fund

Success stories on urban growth management and air quality improvement:
- Internet (search under "growth management," "sprawl," "air quality," etc.; search also for Portland, Oregon, and Chattanooga, Tennessee, as these two cities have been highlighted in many articles for their relatively successful response to this issue)
- Environmental magazines such as *E Magazine, Orion Afield* and *National Wildlife*
- Periodical search at your local library for newspaper articles on this issue

Transportation and air quality issues in your area:
- Local daily and weekly newspapers (collect articles far in advance of the unit, if possible)
- Local NGOs, such as those working on air quality issues or transportation alternatives
- Your state or provincial department of transportation
- Your local transit authority
- Any local commissions developed to address transportation issues

Review newspaper articles carefully to identify other decision-makers and stakeholders.

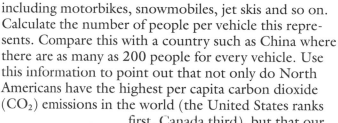

Counting the Real Costs of Cars

An activity for high school students and adults

In this activity, students will use a method called "full cost assessment" to compare several vehicles on the basis of their costs of ownership and their contributions to the climate change problem. Students will gain an understanding of the economic and environmental costs of owning a vehicle.

Concepts

☞ The full cost assessment of a vehicle purchase reveals the many hidden costs, both environmental and financial.

☞ Transportation choices are an important factor in our personal environmental impact.

☞ Transportation is a major source of greenhouse gases.

Objectives

When they have completed this activity, students should be able to:

☞ Conduct an abbreviated full cost assessment to compare the value of vehicles being considered for purchase.

☞ Describe a process for calculating the lifetime carbon dioxide emissions from a vehicle.

☞ Describe the process of assessing the full costs of other consumer products besides cars.

Resources and materials

☞ Fact Sheet: The Facts on Cars, Carbon and Climate Change (see page 52)

☞ Student Worksheet: "Calculating the Costs of Vehicle Ownership" (see page 50)

Preparation

Students may conduct this activity as a field research project or use data that you provide.

Activity plans

Introduction

Conduct a quick class survey of the total number of fossil-fuel-powered vehicles owned by students' families,

Hamish Wilson

including motorbikes, snowmobiles, jet skis and so on. Calculate the number of people per vehicle this represents. Compare this with a country such as China where there are as many as 200 people for every vehicle. Use this information to point out that not only do North Americans have the highest per capita carbon dioxide (CO_2) emissions in the world (the United States ranks first, Canada third), but that our transportation habits are responsible for a very large proportion of the greenhouse gases we produce.

Brainstorm all the ways that cars affect the environment and create an "effects web" to illustrate that they have costs and environmental impacts far beyond their day-to-day operating costs. Include upstream impacts such as pollution from the production of fuels and metals, as well as downstream impacts connected with the disposal of car components such as batteries and air conditioners. Explain full cost assessment as the notion of defining costs so as to include all those associated with the manufacture, use and disposal of a product.

Introduce the idea of comparing three vehicles on the basis of their purchase and operating costs and their emissions of CO_2, the principal greenhouse gas. Organize the class into project teams that will each research three vehicles. Teams may be assigned different sizes and classes of vehicles, such as sport utility vehicles, luxury cars and light trucks.

Calculating the costs

Distribute copies of the worksheet "Calculating the Costs of Vehicle Ownership" and explain that values in the worksheet indicated by "input" must be researched by the project teams. Sources for this data include sales representatives at local car dealerships, new vehicle buyers' guides, Natural Resources Canada *Fuel Efficiency Guide for New Vehicles* (or equivalent publication), and other publications such as Phil Edmonston's *Lemon Aid*, a guide to used cars.

Once the data is gathered, each team works through the step-by-step calculations on the worksheet.

Calculating the Costs of Vehicle Ownership

Vehicle Data

	Make	input			
	Model	input			
	Engine Size (L)	input			
	Fuel Type	gas or diesel			
	Retail Price (includes tax)	input			

Operating Costs

a	Fuel Efficiency (L/100 km)	input			
b	Annual Mileage (km)	assume 24,000	24,000	24,000	24,000
c	Fuel Price ($/L)	input			
d	Annual Fuel Consumption (L)	b x a ÷ by 100			
e	Annual Fuel Costs	c x d			
f	Annual Maintenance Costs	input			
g	Annual Insurance Premium	input			
h	Vehicle Registration Fee	input			
i	Other Annual Fees	input			
j	Total Annual Operating Costs	e + f + g + h + i			
k	Operating Costs Over 4 Years	4 x j			
l	Daily Operating Costs	j ÷ 365			

Ownership Costs

m	Down Payment	input			
n	Monthly Payments	input			
o	Term (number of payments)	assume 48	48	48	48
p	Financed Cost Over 4 Years	m + (n x o)			
q	Daily Cost of Ownership	p ÷ (365 x 4)			

CO_2 Emissions

r	Tailpipe CO_2 Emission Factor	select from below			
s	Annual Exhaust CO_2 Emissions (kg)	d x r			
t	Upstream CO_2 Emission Factor	select from below			
u	Annual Upstream Emissions (kg)	d x t			
v	Total Annual Emissions (kg)	s + u			
w	Emissions Over 4 Years (kg)	v x 4			

Summary

x	Total Costs Over 4 Years	k + p			
y	Average Daily Cost Over 4 Years	x ÷ (365 x 4)			
z	Average Daily CO_2 Over 4 Years	v ÷ 365			

CO_2 Emission Factors

CO_2 Source	Gasoline	Diesel
Tailpipe CO_2 Emissions from Fuel Combustion (kg/L)	2.36	2.77
Upstream CO_2 Emissions from Fuel Production (kg/L)	0.65	0.54

The CO_2 Emission Factors are estimates of how much CO_2 is released during the production and combustion of the fuels used by vehicles.

Transportation

The formulas may be entered in a spreadsheet program to speed up the calculations. The CO₂ Emission Factors at the bottom of the worksheet give estimates of how much carbon dioxide is released during the production (upstream emissions) and combustion (tailpipe emissions) of the fuels used by the vehicles.

Processing the results

When the students have finished their calculations, the data may be organized and presented in various ways:

↝ Rank the vehicles according to operating costs, costs of ownership and carbon dioxide emissions.

↝ Group the costs and emissions by vehicle category (family vans, sport utility vehicles, compact sedans, full-size passenger cars, trucks, etc.).

↝ Prepare bar charts to graphically represent the grouped and ranked data.

Follow-up discussion

The following questions may be the basis for individual or group work or class discussion.

1. Together as a class, rank the vehicles surveyed in order of popularity and preference (not fuel efficiency). Compare this ranking with their ranking on the basis of fuel efficiency and cost. How are the lists different, and what factors determine the relative popularity of different models?

2. Is it realistic to expect that young people will place their priority on fuel economy when purchasing new vehicles? Why or why not?

3. What are the barriers to wide acceptance of electric vehicles or other "zero emissions" vehicles? How important are perception and image in the marketing of domestic vehicles?
An important barrier to wide acceptance of zero-emissions vehicles will likely be their high initial cost. These vehicles will depend on exotic technologies such as high tech batteries, flywheels or hydrogen fuel cells. They may, in the interest of reducing aerodynamic drag, have unconventional body designs, which may be difficult for consumers to accept.

4. One strategy suggested to curb greenhouse gas emissions is for governments to assess a special charge on fossil fuels or other greenhouse gas-emitting

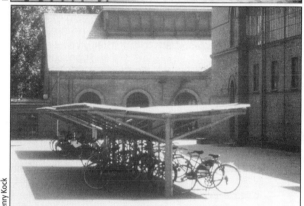

Top: Staff parking lot, Canada.
Bottom: Staff parking lot, Denmark.

Hamish Wilson

Henry Kock

technologies. How might this affect preferences for new vehicles?
A greenhouse gas emission charge will raise the cost of buying fuel, which will give people incentives either to buy more fuel-efficient cars or to drive their vehicles less often. This plan could also make alternative transportation such as public transit much more attractive.

5. Make a list of the environmental impacts associated with vehicles besides greenhouse gas emissions. Try to agree on which impacts are most important in your area. Suggest ways of reducing these impacts.

6. The choice between purchasing high- and low-efficiency vehicles has a relatively marginal impact on greenhouse gas emissions compared with the impact of avoiding the use of cars altogether. Describe several transportation alternatives. For each, identify the associated environmental and social benefits and costs.

Extension ideas

1. Use the results of the research on vehicle efficiency and costs to create a display for the school, a regional education conference or the local mall.

2. How much could you reduce your costs and personal greenhouse gas emissions by not owning a car? What lifestyle adjustments would be needed to get by without a vehicle?

3. Extend the concept of full cost assessment to compare other items. For example, compare:

↝ electric and natural-gas hot water heaters

↝ ethanol-blended and regular gasoline

↝ incandescent light bulbs and equivalent compact fluorescent bulbs

↝ light rail transit and diesel buses for urban mass transit ⸙

This activity and accompanying fact sheet are adapted from "Cars and Climate — Counting the Cost" in Climate Change: Awareness and Action Education Kit *by the Pembina Institute for Appropriate Development in Drayton Valley, Alberta (see Organization and Resources section).*

The Facts on Cars, Carbon, and Climate Change

Our Automobile Addiction

North Americans are addicted to cars. Most of us depend on motorized transport every day. We use cars to go to work, take a vacation, earn a living, or simply to go buy groceries. In fact, we find it hard to imagine life without cars.

In Canada, there is roughly one car for every two people, and many homes have more than one car. Once the purchase cost, insurance, registration, fuel, repairs and traffic tickets are added up, the average Canadian car owner spends approximately $8,000 a year to own and operate a car. This is more money than the average spent on food, housing, or education in a year. In the United States, it has been estimated that drivers spend an average of 1,600 hours per year either driving in their cars, working to cover the cost of owning and operating the car, or working to pay the income and fuel taxes that are used to build the road system. That is equal to 200 eight-hour days, all dedicated to the car.

Clearly, our addiction to cars is serious, and we will go to great lengths to satisfy it. And just like many addictions, our addiction to the car has a number of nasty side effects.

Cars and Climate Change

Cars are one of the largest single sources of the greenhouse gases that are changing global climate. In North America, the average car produces more than five metric tonnes (11,000 lbs.) of carbon dioxide (CO_2) every year. Passenger cars and trucks produced about 15 percent of Canada's CO_2 emissions in 1994, and about 29 percent of nitrous oxide emissions in 1993. Car air-conditioning systems are one of the biggest sources of emissions of chlorofluorocarbons (CFCs) and hydrofluorocarbons (HFCs). These figures do not include the greenhouse gases produced in the manufacture of cars, or in the exploration, development and refining of the gasoline used to power them.

The contribution of cars to climate change will become even more significant in the future. While transportation makes up only a small percentage of greenhouse gas emissions in many developing countries (e.g., there is only one car for every 455 people in India), this is changing rapidly. Globally, new cars are being put on the road at the rate of one per second. As a result, transportation is the fastest growing source of greenhouse gases in the world.

Other Environmental Impacts of Cars

Air Pollution: Cars contribute to acid rain (nitrogen oxides) and urban smog (nitrogen oxides and hydrocarbons), and release hazardous chemicals such as benzene into the atmosphere.

Death and Injury: Around the world, road accidents kill nearly a million people a year and injure over 10 million.

Wilderness Destruction: Automobile infrastructure (highways, roads, driveways, parking lots) makes up nearly 50 percent of the surface area of most North American cities.

Oil Spills: Most oil is produced to fuel automobiles, and transporting that oil causes damage to waterways. Since 1990, an average of 100,000 metric tonnes of oil have been spilled each year worldwide, amounting to the equivalent of 30 *Exxon Valdez* accidents.

Waste Disposal: As an example, 230 million tires need to be disposed of in the United States each year.

Climate-Friendly Transportation

If we are to reduce greenhouse gas emissions, we must break our addiction to the automobile. In the short term, this means using other modes of transportation whenever possible. A person driving alone in a car produces about eight times as much CO_2 as someone taking public transit. Bicycles are one of the most Earth-friendly modes of transportation. They use no fuels and produce virtually no pollution. Repairing and maintaining them requires simple tools and skills. Bicycle routes are far less costly than roads and highways to build and maintain. A final bonus is that bicycles are easy to recycle when they can no longer be used.

In countries like Canada and the United States, choosing modes of transport other than automobiles is not always simple. Our cities have been designed around the car. Few of us live close to where we work, shop or play. In Europe, cities are much more dense (there are more people and services in each square kilometer), making alternative modes of transportation more attractive. In fact, it has been shown that people living in large North American cities use four times as much energy for transportation as people living in large European cities. Breaking our dependence on cars in the long term will require us to redesign our cities so that alternative modes of transportation will be more attractive and cars much less necessary.

Reducing the Impact of Today's Cars on Global Climate

While it is relatively easy for most North Americans to reduce their use of the car, many will still want to own one. Cost, color and style are some of the things people consider when buying a car. To protect global climate, however, we also need to consider fuel efficiency. Buying fuel-efficient cars makes both economic and environmental sense. When less fuel is burned, less greenhouse gas is produced and costs to the driver are lower. As illustrated below, these differences can be substantial:

Fuel Economy (L/100 km)	CO_2 Emissions (20,000 km/yr)	Fuel Cost (@$0.70/L)
8.7	4.1 tonnes	$1,218
6.0	2.8 tonnes	$ 840

Tomorrow's Cars

Is it possible to build a climate-friendly car? Doing so will require us to abandon gasoline as a motor fuel. While some alternative-fuel vehicles exist (e.g., natural gas, propane, and hybrids using both electricity and gasoline), these vehicles still use fossil fuels and produce greenhouse gas emissions. The outlook is very good for climate-friendly transportation. For example, technologies have been developed which make ethanol (the same fuel used in high-performance race cars) from biomass such as wood and agricultural wastes. Using ethanol as a vehicle fuel produces CO_2, but the crops used to make the ethanol would take just as much or more CO_2 out of the atmosphere. Until we find a substitute for the internal combustion engine, ethanol and other biomass fuels may be a good interim solution.

At the moment, work continues on several alternatives to fossil fuels for transportation. Engineers have demonstrated cars powered by electricity and by hydrogen fuel cells, both of which emit no significant greenhouse gases during their operation. As long as the electricity used to charge them up comes from renewable sources (such as solar, hydroelectric or wind), these vehicles will be the climate-friendly choices of the future.

Taking Action on Climate Change: Inside and Outside our Schools

by Denise Philippe and Richard Kool

Mention climate change and some people's first reaction is uncertainty about what it means. Others know what it means but wonder whether we need to be concerned about it or doubt that it is occurring at all. For many educators, the question is not whether climate change is occurring, as the scientific data is compelling enough to convince us that it is. Rather, the question is how to engage students in meaningful exploration of this global issue and in positive action within their own communities.

Climate change is difficult to address tangibly, due in part to its relative invisibility. But it is the slow pace of climate change — the long period over which it manifests itself — that largely accounts for people's natural reluctance to recognize and respond to it. "Natural" because, as ecologist Paul Erlich has pointed out, our vertebrate nervous system has evolved as a "fight or flight" mechanism: it is built to respond to sudden changes or threats in our environment but not to changes that develop slowly and incrementally. This makes it difficult for us to perceive climate change as a threat, since it is a slowly emerging phenomenon which began more than a generation before us and may not reach truly crisis proportions until at least a generation after us.

For students, comprehending the time period over which climate change occurs is not the only challenge. They may also struggle to make sense of climate change in the absence of direct experience, and its global scale can prevent them from feeling that they have any ability to effect change. One way to bring the topic into focus is to use the school as a starting point, allowing students to explore how our local environments — in this case the local "school-scape" — are part of the problem, and can be part of the solution. Taking steps to make schools more energy-efficient will not only demonstrate positive local action but also provide direct learning possibilities. In the following we suggest some ways that teachers can involve students in addressing climate change through activities, both inside and outside of the school, that have real environmental impact and educational value.

Destination Conservation

Students initiate a "lights off" campaign to reduce their school's carbon emissions and utility costs.

The indoor environment

Much of our day is spent in built environments that use huge amounts of natural resources, both in their construction and, more importantly for us, in their daily operation. In schools, three areas of resource use that are directly linked to greenhouse gas emissions, and hence to climate change, are the consumption of electricity and water and the generation of waste:

Electricity: Schools use vast amounts of electricity each year, nearly every kilowatt coming from coal, natural gas and hydroelectric plants that discharge greenhouse gases into the atmosphere. While the generation of hydroelectric power creates little greenhouse gas, the construction of dams does, and the consequent flooding of forest land reduces the ability of the environment to absorb and sequester carbon dioxide (CO_2). Recent research points out that decomposing vegetation in valleys flooded by dams also releases significant amounts of methane, another potent greenhouse gas.[1]

Water: Few of us associate water with greenhouse gases, but that is simply because we are not thinking of our water taps as part of a system. Water is usually pumped from a source and treated with chemicals before we use it, and pumped and treated again before it is put back into the environment. All this movement and treatment of water takes energy, and producing this energy contributes to greenhouse gas emissions.

Waste: The link between consumable materials and climate change is clear: everything we purchase has taken energy to produce. Single-use materials — and schools are full of them — result in greenhouse gas emissions both in their production and, if they are simply thrown away after use, in their decomposition in landfills.

While it is possible to address energy, water and waste separately, a project that addresses all three areas of resource use is likely to be more effective in the long run. Many organizations and individuals provide audits and consultations to help schools develop such programs. For example, Destination Conservation (Canada) and the Green Schools Program of the Alliance to Save Energy (U.S.) both offer training and assistance to help schools reduce their environmental impact and operating costs.[2]

The best of such programs involve schools in a two-prong attack on reducing greenhouse gas emissions. The first stage is to carry out technical audits of the school's operations and to propose low-cost or no-cost technical changes that have the potential to reduce both the use of natural resources and the amount of money spent to operate the school. The second essential aspect of a conservation program is environmental education, the aim of which is to help students and staff make changes that will result in a more resource-efficient school "lifestyle." Implemented together, these strategies can result in huge savings, reducing the emission of greenhouse gases by tonnes of CO_2 per year and at the same time saving thousands of dollars in utility bills.

School-wide energy and resource conservation projects also have significant educational potential. For example, using CO_2 calculators[3] and data collected from utility bills, students can determine how much CO_2 would have been generated by the school, and per capita, had they not reduced their consumption of natural resources. Due to the quantitative

While it is possible to address energy, water and waste separately, a project that addresses all three areas of resource use is likely to be more effective in the long run.

Destination Conservation

Caught in the washroom again – monitoring water use at school.

nature of the project, whereby students are made aware of the savings in both dollars and in quantities of resources, they can clearly see the impact of their actions.

The outdoor environment

Much of a school's potential energy savings and CO_2 reduction will come from measures taken inside the building. However, proper design of the school grounds can also reduce energy consumption. At the same time, it provides opportunities for students to learn about other problems associated with climate change such as habitat change and the link between vegetation and the regulation of temperature in buildings.

Planting trees close to the school building reduces the need for air conditioning in the warmer months and provides an extra barrier to heat loss during the winter. Deciduous trees planted on the south side of building have the additional benefit of allowing sunlight to enter the classrooms in winter, reducing the need to keep lights on during the day. Another way to use school landscaping to address climate change is by planting rooftop gardens. These gardens act as an extra insulating layer, reducing both the heating and cooling needs of the building.

Rooftop gardens can also significantly reduce the urban "heat island" effect. When the sun is directly overhead in summer, asphalt and concrete surfaces absorb the sun's heat during the day and radiate it at night. As a result, urban areas are generally hotter in summertime than the surrounding countryside and people are compelled to increase their use of air conditioning. Replacing heat-absorbing surfaces with gardens helps to ameliorate this effect and reduce energy consumption during warm summer months.

The choice of plant material is a further consideration. Using native plants will reduce or eliminate the need for fertilizers which are a source of nitrous oxide. Replacing turf surfaces with native trees, shrubs and ground cover also lowers fuel consumption by eliminating the need to mow these areas. An added bonus is a reduction in watering once the plants establish themselves (after the first two years) because native plants are well adapted to regional rainfall patterns.

Gardens and natural areas are also good sites for exploring the relationship between climate and plant and animal habitat. One concern raised about climate change is that plants that have adapted over thousands of years to a specific climate zone may not be able to tolerate, and will not have time to adapt to, temperature or rainfall variances that are beyond their biogeoclimatic zone limits. In designing a school nature area, students will need to select a community of plants best adapted to the conditions of their site. From there they may move up the spatial scale to explore biogeoclimatic zones, coming to understand that plants and animals depend on a specific range of temperatures, sunlight and precipitation. Climate change effects are frequently presented as large-scale phenomena, from violent storms to melting ice caps and rising sea levels; but changes in climate may also alter the composition of local ecosystems. This is an opportunity to explore some of the questions that face climate-change researchers today: What are the means by which plant species adapt to changing environmental conditions? How quickly can they adapt? What would be the ecological, economic and social impact of large-scale die-off in a species that cannot adapt quickly enough? A related question posed by various earth and atmospheric science researchers is whether climate change will reduce biodiversity. While we do not yet know the answer to this, we do know that biogeoclimatic zones will change as higher temperatures encourage the migration of plants and animals to more northern latitudes and higher elevations. This shift may quite radically affect ecological relationships within and among various habitats, as well as humans' relationships with the local environment. Helping students make the link between local habitats and climate conditions, and the evolving risks to plant, animal and even human communities as a result of climate change, can be an important function of any naturalization project.

And finally, let's not forget the potential of school gardens to teach students about the relationship between food production and climate change. Here in British Columbia, much of our produce comes from places far away. Mangoes are trucked in from Mexico, potatoes may travel by train from Idaho, and tomatoes may be flown in from California. Using road maps and the on-line climate change calculator, students can compare the impact of an imported tomato with that of a locally grown tomato. How many different CO_2-emitting modes of transportation were used to get the tomato to the table? How much CO_2 was created? Certainly, reducing the distance our food travels by growing food locally is an important and immediate action we can all take. Food gardens, whether on the

Michelle Doucet

Planting a green barrier to winter cold and summer heat.

roof or on the school ground, offer students at the same time an opportunity to develop better nutritional habits and a better understanding of how much agriculture relies on the predictability of weather.

The initiatives described above are as much action-oriented as they are about generating awareness and understanding of the many facets of climate change. As such, they are about "grounding" this global, atmospheric phenomenon in a way that makes tangible sense to students. Balancing knowledge, awareness and understanding with action is essential, for if we fail to show students ways that each of us can make a difference, we risk engendering feelings of hopelessness or paralysis when we teach about the large-scale, long-term nature of climate change. Turning off a light or planting a shade tree may seem a small gesture, but students can readily understand that even such small, incremental changes do have tangible results: less energy used really does equal less greenhouse gas emitted.

If we do nothing and instead let ourselves drift into a climate change crisis, it will likely be too late for the incremental changes that may still be of value today. We will have backed ourselves into a "fight or flight" predicament; but we will have only ourselves to fight with and, clearly, no other place to fly. We must act now. ◎

Denise Philippe is Program Manager for Western Canada at Evergreen in Vancouver, British Columbia. Richard Kool is the Education/Interpretation Programs Officer for British Columbia Parks in Victoria, British Columbia.

Notes

1. World Commission on Dams, June 2000, http://www.dams.org/press/pressrelease_54.htm.

2. For more information, readers may contact these organizations directly: Destination Conservation, 10511 Saskatchewan Drive, Edmonton, AB T6E 4S1, (780) 433-8711, fax (780) 439 5081, e mail info@dc.ab.ca; The Green Schools Program, The Alliance to Save Energy, 1200 18th Street NW, Suite 900, Washington, DC 20036, (202) 857-0666, fax (202) 331-9588.

3. The University of British Columbia has designed an interactive on-line climate change calculator which students can use to determine the greenhouse gas emissions produced through everyday activities. It can be found at www.climcalc.net.

References

McBean, G. A., and H.G. Hengeveld, H. G. "Communicating the Science of Climate Change: A Mutual Challenge for Scientists and Educators." *Canadian Journal of Environmental Education*, 5, 2000.

Wackernagel, M. and W. Rees, W. *Our Ecological Footprint: Reducing Human Impact on the Earth*. Gabriola Island, BC: New Society Publishers, 1996.

Wackernagel, M., L. Onisto, L., A.C. Linares, I.S.L. Falfn, J.M. Garca, A.I.S. Guerrero, and M.G.S. Guerrero. *Ecological Footprints of Nations: How much nature do they use? How much nature do they have?* San Juan, Costa Rica: The Earth Council, 1997. Also on-line at http://www.redefiningprogress.org.

What Cool Schools Can Do

by Tom Yohemas

Unlike government and industry, some schools are making great progress towards meeting or beating the international goal of reducing carbon dioxide (CO_2) emissions below 1990 levels. A study of 161 Alberta schools involved in the Destination Conservation program revealed that energy conservation measures had reduced the schools' emissions of CO_2 by more than 5,576 metric tonnes and had saved $457,399 in utility expenditures over a one-year period. Clearly, the reduction of greenhouse gases can lead to substantial economic as well as environmental benefits.

The following are activities that students, teachers and staff can undertake to save energy and reduce carbon emissions. Most topics are divided into two parts: no-cost activities that students and staff can undertake, and technical initiatives that need to be implemented by maintenance and custodial staff. As you will discover, the possibilities are limited only by the imagination of your school community.

David Dodge

Toilet paper, tape and a pencil — the only tools needed to perform a draft-proofing audit at school.

Electricity

Electricity typically represents about 60 percent of a school's total utility budget.

- Invite guest speakers from local utility companies to promote conservation at school assemblies.
- Monitor the school's utility bills to track changes in energy use.
- Set up a bulletin board display showing the school's energy use and the potential savings through conservation and retrofitting.
- Start an Electric Police or Powerbusters Club to encourage energy conservation.
- Have students audit equipment in the school, checking for energy efficiency and proper maintenance.

Computers

- Install energy-efficient screen savers on your computers.
- Turn off computers during lunch breaks, after school, on weekends and any other time they are not in use.
- When buying printers or other computer hardware, check their efficiency on the EnergyGuide (Canada) or Green Star (U.S.) labels.

Photocopiers and laminators

Photocopiers and laminators consume large amounts of electricity and produce unwanted heat.

- Use an overhead master for exam questions.
- Purchase photocopiers with energy-saver standby functions.
- Turn off photocopiers at night, on weekends and on holidays.
- To reduce peak demand loads, use laminators only when other equipment such as kilns and photocopiers are not running. Better yet, try to reduce your use of this energy pig.
- Limit staff to a certain number of photocopies per year to reduce electricity and paper costs. Staff can brainstorm alternatives with their students or environment club members.

Technical controls

- Reduce peak demand loads by scheduling air handling units to go on when other machinery is inactive.
- Install control systems that can shed or shift lower priority electrical loads to minimize their effect on peak demand.
- Install variable speed motors in large fan units that do not always need to run at full output.

Heating systems

- Examine windows and exterior doors and report drafts to your maintenance department.
- Encourage the closing of exterior doors by having students make presentations and classroom visits.

The School Building

- In the colder months designate a student or staff member to close the curtains at night to conserve heat and to open them during the day for solar warmth and natural light.

- Launch a "Heat Down" campaign which includes a "Sweater Day" for students and staff.

Technical controls

- Ensure that the school's furnaces are computer-controlled for energy efficiency.

- Insulate hot water pipes and hot water tanks to reduce energy consumption.

- Ensure that insulation is upgraded to current standards during renovations or retrofits.

- Install timers on thermostats to turn heat down at night, on weekends or during holidays when the school is closed.

- Consider installing solar walls on the south side of the building, thus using passive solar energy to heat outside air for use inside the school.

- Install a building automation system to control the heating. These systems monitor outdoor air temperature and supply heat only as needed. They can also be scheduled to heat only when the building is occupied.

Lighting

Lighting consumes 60 percent of the electricity used in the average school.

- Keep hall lights off in the morning until students arrive.

- Put tape over the switches of lights that are not needed.

- Start a "Lights Off" campaign so that lights are not used during sunny days or in rooms that are not occupied.

Technical controls

- Reduce lighting in overlit areas. Excessive lighting can cause headaches and is associated with hyperactivity in some children.

- Replace exit lights with L.E.D. exit panels that use less than two volts.

- Arrange for a lighting retrofit or include it in modernization plans. New T-8 fluorescent lamps and electronic ballasts are, on average, 24 percent more efficient, provide a more natural light and have a longer life span than standard fluorescent lighting. They are also quieter and have no visible flicker.

- Install motion sensors in washrooms so that lights, and water pumps on urinals, operate only when there is an occupant.

- Install skylights as a means of increasing the use of free, natural light.

- Install switch timers in storage closets. These will automatically turn off the lights after a preset time period.

Transportation

- Take an annual climate change poll at your school. Ask students and staff how they get to school each day and how far they travel. Graph the results, showing the

---

How to calculate your school's CO₂ emissions (An exercise for the very ambitious)

WHILE IT IS POSSIBLE TO CALCULATE your school's annual contribution to global warming, it does require a bit of research. Here's how to get started.

To compare your school's carbon dioxide (CO_2) emissions in 1990 and 2000, for example, start by obtaining copies of the utility bills for these periods. These should be available from your maintenance department, school board office or local utility company. Both electricity and heating fuel contribute directly to the accumulation of greenhouse gases, so both should be evaluated.

By calculating the total energy or fuel consumed each year and multiplying it by a conversion factor, you will be able to determine the amount of CO_2 produced. For instance, the calculation for natural gas is gigajoules x 0.05916667 = tonnes CO_2. The CO_2 conversion factors must be obtained from your local utility because they are specific to the fuel used and to the units in which consumption is measured (some natural gas bills show consumption as units of energy, others show it as a volume of gas).

The conversion factor for electricity depends on the resource that is used for generating it. For example, in Alberta where 85% of electricity is generated from soft coal the conversion equation for electricity is kilowatt-hours x 0.00009838 = tonnes CO_2. The equation will be different in regions where most electricity is produced from nuclear energy, oil or hydroelectric power. You will need to research the sources of your electricity and ask your local utility company to provide the corresponding conversion equation.

More precise results are obtained by normalizing the data for each year, taking into account factors such as weather variations, changes in the size of the school population, and building renovations.

A detailed analysis can become quite complicated and, for most schools, is unnecessary. The main point of initiating action on climate change is not to determine exact emissions levels but to implement day-to-day solutions to reduce our contribution to the problem.

— *Tom Yohemas*

percentages of people who walk, bike, drive or take public transit. Research the average fuel efficiencies of cars and buses in your area. Using the statistic that vehicles release 2.35 kilograms of carbon dioxide for every liter of gasoline consumed (18.8 pounds per US gallon), determine the total amount of carbon dioxide released by these vehicles in their daily trips to and from school. Graph the emissions of each transport group and post these in the school's main hallway. Repeat this poll each year and make comparisons with previous years.

- Publicize the environmental benefits of public transit. Make posters comparing the different public space requirements of cars, buses and bicycles. Cooperate with local transit authorities to develop advertisements for public transit.

- Discourage parents and school bus drivers from idling their engines in front of the school.

- Encourage carpooling among teachers and older students to save energy and reduce fuel bills and CO_2 emissions.

- Start a bicycle club. Have older students teach bike maintenance to younger students. Sell bike helmets as a fundraiser.

- In northern regions where school parking lots have electrical outlets for engine block heaters, use "flip flop" controls that charge only half of the cars at any given moment. Alternatively, vehicles could be plugged in manually by students only when temperatures drop.

- Charge a small fee for parking in the school lot and use the money for treeplanting and other environmental projects.

Treeplanting

As carbon sinks which take up and store atmospheric carbon, trees play a major role in reducing greenhouse gases.

- Celebrate Arbor Day or May Day with guest speakers and treeplanting to promote community greening.

- Research the importance of protecting rainforests as a means of conserving one of the Earth's largest carbon sinks. The burning of rainforests directly releases massive amounts of CO_2, and the replacement of rainforest vegetation with food crops or grass for grazing seriously reduces the planet's carbon storage capacity.

- Adopt a tree in your community.

- Plant deciduous trees on the south side of the school to cool the building and reduce the need for air conditioning during warm months.

- Plant coniferous trees on the north and west sides of the school to reduce the impact of cold winter winds and reduce heating demand.

- Support wilderness protection, since the vegetation in natural areas absorbs greenhouse gases.

Water Use

Reducing water usage also reduces the energy required for pumping and purifying it.

- Have students survey how much water is used in the school and brainstorm how it can be conserved.

- Eliminate lawn watering by landscaping with native species that require little water.

- Place plastic bottles in toilet tanks to reduce water use.

- Ask local restaurants to serve water only upon request.

Technical controls

- Install low-flow shower heads to save water and reduce the amount of energy used to heat water.

- Retrofit plumbing to reduce inefficiencies in the use and heating of water.

- Place timers on the boys' urinals to reduce usage of water and electricity. Install water dams in toilets, as they reduce water consumption by 30 percent.

Renewable Energy

Using alternative sources of energy such as wind and solar reduces our use of fossil fuels.

- Create displays on energy-efficient homes as part of a science fair to educate parents and staff about solar power, insulation, caulking and weatherstripping.

- Make simple solar cookers and food dryers to demonstrate a sustainable means of preparing food.

- Install solar water heaters as part of a retrofit or renovation of the school.

- Contact local renewable energy groups for advice and information.

Recycling

Recycling metal, paper, glass and other materials into new products requires less energy than making the same products from new materials.

- Purchase school supplies made from recycled materials.

- Encourage paper recycling to reduce the need to cut carbon-storing trees.

- Ask school district authorities to agree to return a portion of the money saved in reducing the school's paper use. Use the funds to support environmental projects.

Tom Yohemas is the Communications Coordinator for Destination Conservation in Edmonton, Alberta.

Getting Into Hot Water

A hands-on home and school activity that promotes energy and water conservation

by Joe Umanetz

How many of us know a lot about what we "should" do as far as energy conservation goes, but do little about it? Most, I would guess. For our students, the ramifications of squandering energy are even more remote because they don't directly pay the bills, and warnings of the long term implications of almost anything bad for them, from smoking cigarettes to dropping out of school, are voices from a dream. The following assignment brings the importance of energy conservation closer to home — literally — by asking students to calculate the energy they and their families use for baths and showers. You get a few phone calls at first when you drag parents into the educational process, but most welcome the opportunity, especially if the assignment is well designed and relevant to adults. Energy conservation activities fill the bill quite nicely.

Paul Papin

an opportunity to transfer a scaled profile of the tub onto graph paper and teach the same approximating skills one would use for profiling the cross-section of a stream or river. It gets a bit tricky at the ends of the tub because there is a double curve, but profiling can be done in sections and the separate volumes put together as a composite.

An easier method is to time how long it takes to fill a graduated bucket and then calculate how much water is used for a bath or shower by timing how long the water is run. For the bath, an alternative method is to bucket cold water to the desired level, marking volumes incrementally on a piece of white adhesive tape that is stuck to the tub. This method gives a better appreciation of how much water is actually used for a bath. Having a graduated tub also allows data to be taken for all family members.

If possible, students should measure the temperature of incoming cold water, as well as the "just right" temperature of the shower or bath. The cold water temperature can best be determined by allowing the tap to run for a few minutes at the faucet closest to where the water comes into the building. (Readings of incoming cold temperatures will be a little high if the student lives in an apartment because the water will have had to wend its way along a lot of pipe in heated space before reaching the faucet.) Does the coldest temperature possible from the tap vary according to the time of day or the season? Do family members' "just-right" bath temperatures vary? According to what? Does the number of baths or showers taken vary with the time of the week or the time of year? Students can set up a little chart in their bathrooms to record this information.

This activity will have much greater significance if students collect their own data because the results will be specific and personal. However, make sure you do all these things yourself first to get an appreciation of the nitty-gritty details.

Assignment: How much does it cost you to take a bath or shower?

Classroom preparation

Discuss what the students will have to do and know in order to determine the cost of a bath or shower. They will have to find out how much water is used, how much energy is used to heat it, and the cost of both the water and the energy. I provide basic arithmetic data to younger students, but the older ones have to find and develop it on their own. Buckets and thermometers may need to be loaned to students on a rotating basis.

What the students do

I like to leave students to their own devices to determine how to measure the volume of water they use for a typical shower and bath. Just allowing the tub to fill up to a certain level, and using length x width x depth doesn't work well because the sides of the tub are curved. This is

Calculations

After all the data is collected, two sets of calculations must be done. Determining the cost of the water is as simple as multiplying the number of cubic meters or gallons used by the unit cost. To determine the energy cost, first calculate how much energy was used to heat the shower and bath water (see basic data in sidebar). Then convert these units of heat (joules or BTUs) into the energy units used by your utility (kilowatt-hours, therms, or cubic meters of gas), and multiply by the unit cost of the energy.

So what?

In most homes, especially those with electric water heaters, heating water costs more energy dollars by far than any other household activity except for space heating and cooling. A typical family of four uses about 5,500 kilowatt-hours (kwh) annually to heat water and most of this is for showers and baths. These 5,500 kwh are out of a total electrical consumption of about 12,200 kwh which does not include space heating or cooling. (It should be noted that our typical family has not done much in the way of energy conservation.) At 10 to 20 cents per kwh, water heating represents a financial expenditure of $550 to $1,100 per year. It also amounts to a quantity of pollutants whose costs are "externalized" to the commons (air, water, soil) and to other generations (see extension activity below).

When students measure the energy and the financial costs of their baths and showers there is some powerful learning going on:

➪ Students gain confidence by applying skills of measurement and calculation to address real problems and derive real and useful solutions. This aspect of the project is adaptable because the teacher can decide what information the students receive as "given."

➪ Students develop awareness by quantifying part of the environmental impact of one of their everyday actions. Former students have told me — in one case, 12 years later — that visions of energy conservation are among their shower dreams.

➪ Students really can do something about their families' energy use, and in so doing gain status in their homes by saving their parents hundreds of dollars per year at today's energy costs. With low-flow shower heads, aerators and finger-tip valves (available in inexpensive water conservation kits), hot water consumption can easily be cut in half with no loss of performance. If families also superinsulate the hot water tank and pipes, they can reduce hot water costs by up to 90 percent. Finally, hanging a waterproof shower clock from the shower head can help family members keep track of the length of their showers.

Follow-up

As a follow-up, students can measure their post-conservation shower costs. Which low-flow shower heads give a decent shower? How much hot water is used elsewhere? Did the conservation program make a difference in the meter reading? Is there anything that can be done if everybody takes baths instead of showers? Where does the hot water go? Could the heat be retrieved?

Extensions

Home Electricity Audit: Have students check the wattage of all lights and appliances in their homes and then poll their family members to find out how long each appliance is used each day. By reading their household's electricity meter at 24-hour intervals, students can compare their estimated daily consumption of electricity with the actual consumption, and determine the cost of each day's electricity. Students can make recommendations about how to reduce electricity consumption. Which would likely have the greatest impact? Which are most likely to succeed?

Exploring Environmental Impacts: Assess the environmental cost of the natural gas or electricity used to heat water and power the home's lights and appliances. Start by investigating the sources and the means of distribution for each form of energy used in the home. What pollutants and solid wastes were created in producing and distributing this energy? How much CO_2 was emitted? (Contact local utilities to obtain CO_2 conversion factors for the energy sources used to generate your electricity.) §

Joe Umanetz is a Creative Learning Teacher with the Bruce Grey Catholic District School Board in Hanover, Ontario.

On-line resources

Rocky Mountain Institute, www.rmi.org: one of the best sources of information on energy conservation.

Real Goods, www.realgoods.com: a great place to learn about innovative conservation hardware.

Watts on Schools, http://www.wattsonschools.com/calc-chem.htm: a student-friendly calculator that gives the kwh-equivalents of various types of energy (chemical, mechanical, thermal, etc.)

Base data and derivative information

➮ Electric hot water heaters are 100% efficient. (Not taking into account standby and distribution losses which are typically about 25% for any type of tank heater).

➮ Gas water heaters are typically 70% efficient.

➮ Water typically comes into the house at 15°C (60°F); shower and bath water is typically 40°C (104°F).

➮ Contact your local gas, electric and water utilities to obtain the current costs of electricity and natural gas.

Metric units of energy and measure

➮ It takes 4.18 joules of energy to raise 1 ml of water by 1°C

➮ 1 kwh = 3,600,000 joules

➮ 1 cubic meter of natural gas yields 37,470,000 joules

U.S. units of energy and measure

➮ It takes 1 British Thermal Unit (BTU) to raise 1 pound of water by 1°F

➮ 1 gallon (U.S) water weighs 8.34 pounds

➮ 1 kwh = 3,415 BTUs

➮ 1 cubic foot of natural gas yields 1,030 BTUs

➮ 1 therm = 100,000 BTUs

The Clean Air Game

by Deborah Avalone-King

laying the Clean Air Game is a great way to initiate discussion of the importance of protecting the atmosphere and help students understand distinctions between air pollutants and greenhouse gases. The objectives of the game are to acquaint students with sources and types of air pollutants, their impact on the health of people and the environment, and actions individuals can take to prevent air pollution. The game can be used in a number of ways: to spark discussion of how our energy choices create or ameliorate environmental problems; to highlight how non-living aspects of the environment change in response to human and other factors; and to assess the environmental impacts of technology.

Playing the game

The Clean Air Game can be played by students from elementary school (fourth grade) to high school. The suggested play time is 20 to 30 minutes for younger students and 10 to 15 minutes for older students. Additional time is needed for processing and sharing what is learned.

To play the game, students form teams of four or five. Each student has a playing piece and each team has a die. Players start on one of the two Green Spaces and move clockwise around the board. As players land on spaces, they read aloud the description and add or remove pollutants from their atmosphere as directed. When landing on pollutant spaces, players must add one of those pollutants to their atmosphere. (The purpose of these spaces is to familiarize students with the names and chemical abbreviations of pollutants.) Individual players may wish to keep track of their own scores, but the team score is what matters. The team with the lowest score (cleanest air) wins the game.

Scoring can be done on score sheets or by using manipulatives such as pieces of packaged cereals (e.g., "Cheerios" or "Fruit Loops") to represent pollution. When using manipulatives, each student starts the game with 15 pieces of cereal and a handful is placed in the center of the game. To remove pollutants, players eat the cereal pieces. To add pollutants, they take pieces from the center of the board and add them to their own pile.

Scoring strategies can be varied with older students. For example, students may keep a general pollution score with one column for adding pollutants and one column for removing pollutants, and sum it up at the end of the game. Or they may track each of the six pollutants on the board.

Celebrate at the end of the game by rewarding the team that has the cleanest air (least points) with applause or, for fun, a jar of clean air! Have each group share examples of the actions or events that resulted in dirtier air or cleaner air. This reflection is an important way to process the information and better relate the activity to their own lives and the actions they can take to reduce pollution.

Greenhouse gas follow-up

While greenhouse gases are not directly addressed in the game, a follow-up discussion on this topic will enrich students' understanding of the link between air pollution and climate change. Discussion could include:

❧ Are any of the pollutants in the game also greenhouse gases? *(Nitrous oxide and ground-level ozone are called greenhouse gases because they have the ability to absorb and emit heat energy. Some volatile organic compounds undergo a chemical reaction in sunlight to produce ground-level ozone. Ozone has a split personality: in the lower atmosphere it is a heat-trapping pollutant; in the upper atmosphere it forms a layer that shields the Earth from harmful ultraviolet radiation. The "hole" in the ozone layer is not directly related to the greenhouse effect.)*

❧ What major greenhouse gases are not represented on the game board? Why not? *(Carbon dioxide, methane, and chlorofluorocarbons or CFCs are not on the board. Carbon dioxide and methane are produced naturally in the respiration and decomposition of organisms and so have not previously been considered air pollutants. For millions of years, these gases have contributed to the natural greenhouse effect, playing a beneficial role in regulating the Earth's surface temperature. However, human activities such as burning fossil fuels for energy, clearing forests, and raising livestock are rapidly increasing the levels of these gases in the atmosphere. As a result, the greenhouse effect is enhanced and the Earth is getting warmer. CFCs are human-made compounds which are not pollutants at ground level but act as powerful greenhouse gases in the atmosphere: their heat-trapping ability is thousands of times greater than that of carbon dioxide.)*

❧ Which practices or processes represented on the game board result in the emission of carbon dioxide? *(Activities involving the combustion of the carbon-containing materials such as fossil fuels or wood all produce CO_2 emissions.)* ❧

Deborah Avalone-King is an environmental educator with the Maine Department of Environmental Protection in Augusta. The Clean Air Game was developed by Page Keeley.

PARTICULATE MATTER (PM)

Your family reduces their energy use.

BREATHE THE FRESH AIR AND TAKE ANOTHER TURN.

You have a headache from CO or toxic exposure.

Lose one turn.

dry cleaners

Start here
GREEN SPACE
You may remove any one pollutant.

You are careful not to let your car idle for very long.

Remove one CO, PM and VOC from your atmosphere.

Your woodburning stove gives off CO, PM and Toxics.

Add one of each to your atmosphere.

wood stoves

CARBON MONOXIDE (CO)

Your diesel trucks need engine maintenance.

Add one PM and Toxic to your atmosphere.

diesel engines

You burn small, hot fires with seasoned wood in your woodstove.

Remove one PM and Toxic from your atmosphere.

Volcanoes, pollen, forest fires and trees add natural pollutant to the atmosphere.

Lose one turn.

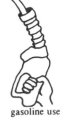
volcanoes, forests

brain damage

gasoline use

contaminated crops

1. Start on a Green Space.
2. Take turns rolling die and moving game pieces. Read aloud and follow instructions on each space you land on. If you land on a pollutant space, add one of that pollutant to your score.
3. Record scores on a tally sheet.
4. The team or player with the lowest score (cleanest air) wins.

smog

reduced alertness

damaged forests

Regional wind patterns carry pollutants long distances.

Take one pollutant from each category and add it to your atmosphere.

You buy a new car that uses an alternative fuel or is a low emissions vehicle.

Remove one O_3 and PM from your atmosphere.

You live near a metal refinery or have found lead paint and pipes in your home.

Add one Pb to your atmosphere.

metal refineries

LE
H
P

You have a coal-burning furnace.

Add one SO$_2$ to your atmosphere.

To reduce acid rain, your local power plant switches to low sulfur coal or oil and installs scrubbers to remove SO$_2$ from your smokestream.

Remove one SO$_2$ from your atmosphere.

You voice your concerns to your legislators.

Every player may remove one pollutant from their atmosphere.

OZONE (O$_3$)

cars

ir Game

heart damage

dead aquatic life

less oxygen in blood

global warming

Every member of your family commutes to work alone each day.

Add one ozone to your atmosphere.

You ride your bike to work each day instead of driving.

Remove one ozone from your atmosphere.

Start here
GREEN SPACE
You may remove any one pollutant.

You can't exercise today because high ozone levels make it difficult to breathe.

Lose one turn.

respiratory problems

---

eye irritation

contaminated livestock

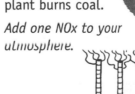
lung damage

The Clean Air Act passes.

BREATHE THE FRESH AIR AND TAKE ANOTHER TURN.

NITROGEN OXIDES and VOLATILE ORGANIC COMPOUNDS (NOx and VOC)

Your sink cabinet and garage contain toxic cleaning solvents and other poisons which increase your risk of cancer.

Lose one turn.

toxic cleaning solvents

You regularly have your car tuned up.

Remove one NOx and O$_3$ from your atmosphere.

Your local power plant burns coal.

Add one NOx to your atmosphere.

electric power plants

Visiting a Sustainable Living Site

Finding and visiting a demonstration site with students

by Barbara Wallace

Energy efficiency, water conservation, species preservation, and recycling are good topics for environmental curriculum units. But what is often missing in this topic-specific approach is a means of integrating all of the suggested actions into a sustainable pattern of living. Kids need to see that there are real, workable and highly satisfying alternatives to our current unsustainable way of life, based on principles of resource conservation, of self-sufficiency and of working within rather than in opposition to the limits of natural systems. In recent years, many real-life examples of sustainable living have arisen around the world in a variety of fascinating settings. These sites include private "sustainable living" homes and farms that are often open for school tours and workshops, more formalized educational centers, and an international network of eco-communities. All provide a rich framework for experiential learning, the examination of lifestyles, and the development of curriculum that excites students.

A visit to a sustainable living site can provide an almost endless number of practical education opportunities for teachers and students. Because these sites offer a non-traditional path into the future, they can be used as a springboard to exploration of the more elusive areas of the curriculum such as values, personal responsibility and system interrelationships. For example, how valuable is efficiency if it destroys soil health, or convenience if it degrades air and water through production or disposal practices? How do you compare material possessions with bird songs, swimmable lakes, and moose ambling through a wetland? The sustainable living approach provides an excellent tool for this type of examination.

Straw bale houses reflect key principles of sustainability: they are energy-efficient dwellings cooperatively constructed from a local and annually renewable resource.

Photos by Barbara Wallace

While each site is unique, each illustrates some of the key principles of sustainable living. These include:

- protecting our life support systems (air, land, and water);
- limiting activities to the carrying capacity of natural systems;
- adopting an ethic based on environmental stewardship and resource conservation;

- meeting the basic needs of material equity and social justice for all members of society;

- meeting social, psychological and spiritual needs through means that minimally rely on material consumption;

- fostering positive relationships between individuals and with nature;

- making optimal use of local resources;

- using materials in continuous cycles; and

- supporting communities to meet their own needs and contribute to the common good while not compromising the sustainability of other communities or generations.

Finding a sustainable living site

Since sustainable living is a relatively new concept, not many locations are fully integrated. You may find that you need to visit several different operations in your area to cover all aspects of sustainable living. A private home or farm operated on principles of sustainability is an ideal site because it provides a clear model of everyday living that students can relate to. Energy-efficient houses ("advanced houses") offer good examples of energy and water conservation. Community and demonstration gardens often interrelate organic food production and species diversity. Other possibilities include alternative technology centers; science centers that have advanced wastewater treatment systems using various organisms, flowering plants, and marshes; and conservation areas and farms that use alternative technologies or are involved in organic growing or the conservation of rare breeds or heritage seeds.

What to look for at a site

A visit to a sustainable living site should introduce students to living, working examples of two important components of sustainability: security and simplicity. Security refers to meeting basic needs for food, air, water, clothing, shelter, emotional involvement, physical and spiritual health, and employment or meaningful activity. At a sustainable living site, security might mean having an independent source of electricity produced by solar, wind or water systems. Or it could mean planting a wide variety of plants so that weather or changes in insect populations will not wipe out the winter's supply of food. Or it could mean preserving rare plants, animals and cultures so that future needs can be met.

Simplicity refers to living in the most efficient, economic and effective way. Choosing simple paths often means examining priorities and finding ways that one new habit or component of living will complement another. For example, a pond fed by a rainwater collection system might provide habitat for many species, an enjoyable location for visiting with friends, a place to cool off on a hot day, and irrigation water for the garden. Simple systems are usually the least expensive and incorporate only those appropriate technological innovations that can be integrated into natural cycles.

A lesson in the recycling of yard and animal wastes.

Two key areas of interest to students are appropriate technologies and food-producing plants and animals. The technologies should incorporate energy efficiency, water conservation and toxics reduction. There should be signage or guides to explain the relevance and construction or operational details of structures, technologies, and systems. For example, at the off-the-electric-grid Sun Run Centre in Cameron, Ontario:

- all operations are powered by solar photovoltaic cells and a wind generator;

- rainwater flows from eaves troughs to a large storage tank to be used for garden watering;

- a plastered straw-bale chicken house keeps the birds warm in the winter and cool in the summer;

- a permanent greenhouse, movable tunnel greenhouses, and cold frames extend the growing season;

- various compost methods are used instead of commercial fertilizers;

- rare Kerry cows provide manure for compost and milk for various dairy products;

- a functional "dry" toilet does not need a septic system connection;
- a solar shower and hand-washing sink provide hot water from the sun;
- a demonstration garden of useful native herbs and flowers surrounds a small pond;
- a herb spiral and extensive interplantings of herbs and vegetables tests various combinations of companion plantings used to stimulate growth or avoid the need for pesticides;
- a passive solar center contains energy-efficient windows, lighting and refrigeration and low-flow water usage;
- large gardens containing a wide variety of species provide an abundance of food; and
- as at most sites, there are also areas for picnicking and relaxing.

Students get a first hand look at passive solar heating.

Curriculum links

The following are a few suggestions which illustrate how you can integrate a visit to a sustainable living site into the curriculum:

Language Arts: Write letters or do research to gather information before visiting the site. Write reports to be sent home to parents explaining what some of the components are and how they are related, describing all the systems at the site or some components that could be used at their home.

Art: Prepare a photographic, pictorial or scale-model version or a video program for display at the school and for a public awareness meeting.

Mathematics: Observe sun coverage of the photovoltaic panels, record the resulting amperage meter readings, and determine how many light bulbs and appliances could be run for how long. Calculate the amount of planting area needed to provide a family of four with potatoes or other vegetables for a year. Determine how many straw bales would be required to build a small cottage.

Science: Study building and landscape design features that would lower energy requirements. Record and analyze plant heights, general health, and amount of useful food production in various companion planting combinations. Design a system for rainwater collection and use at your school.

Geography: Develop a map of the site, taking into account prevailing wind direction, summer and winter solar angles, coniferous and deciduous trees, and access routes. Select several sustainable living components that could be incorporated into your school grounds and map their locations to maximize efficient interrelationships.

A visit to a sustainable living site should introduce students to living, working examples of two important components of sustainability: security and simplicity.

History: Research the history of one or more appropriate technologies, examining the past and current barriers to their development or widespread acceptance. Research living methods of a century ago in your area, compare to present methods, and determine if some older practices might be valuable today. Compare alternative energy, organic food production or energy-efficient buildings and appliances to the related mainstream technologies of mass produced and distributed energy, industrial agriculture, and typical housing and appliances.

Visits to sustainable living sites, accompanied by curriculum activities and direct application in the school or in students' own homes, can increase young people's understanding of environmentally sustainable living practices and strengthen their personal sense of hope for the future. ◈

Barbara Wallace is co-director of the Sun Run Centre for Sustainable Living in Cameron, Ontario.

Cycling for a Better World

*A solidarity ride enables students to take action
on climate change both locally and globally*

by Gilles Bélisle

Can high school students change the world? Our experience at Jean-Baptiste-Meilleur Secondary School in Repentigny, Québec, shows that young people have the will and the power to do just that. Every spring for the last nine years, the students at our school have contributed their time and energy to solidarity rides: annual bike-a-thons whose aim is to build a better world. The interest in this program lies in its double challenge: to raise funds through sponsorships to help a developing country, and at the same time to work locally to improve the well-being and sustainability of the community.

Over the years, we have used several themes for solidarity rides, ranging from drinking water and soil erosion to children's rights. A few years ago, the ride's theme was climate change. The challenge for the students was,

Solidarity ride in Repentigny, Québec.

Photographs by Gilles Bélisle

on the one hand, to raise money to fight desertification in Ghana through the planting of trees, and on the other, to collect signatures on a petition asking the mayor to fast-track the construction of a network of bicycle paths in Repentigny. The outcome: The students' solidarity ride raised $6,000 which was matched by the Canadian International Development Agency and given to an organization that is fighting desertification in Ghana; and their petition gave a major boost to the plans to establish a network of bicycle paths. But beyond the numbers, an entire school had been sensitized to the problem of climate change, its causes and its consequences. A group of young people had understood that, united, we can change things.

Given the enthusiasm shown by both the students and teaching staff for this program, I thought it might be interesting to share my experience, so that — who knows? — perhaps other solidarity rides might be organized in other parts of the world.

Objectives of a solidarity ride

From an educational perspective, the main goal of a solidarity ride is to lead students to:

❧ learn about the causes and consequences of climate change;

❧ learn about the links between climate change and other environmental problems such as deforestation and desertification;

❧ appreciate that since climate change does not respect borders, we must not only do something in our own neighborhood, but also support and assist people in poorer regions of the world;

❧ become involved in the fight against climate change through concrete actions of solidarity.

Getting organized

A solidarity ride can have a tremendous impact on the entire community — provided that it is a success! And to succeed, adequate preparation and lots of organizing are essential. It is a good idea to set up a small cycling committee that includes teachers, students, administrators, parents, professionals and support staff. In addition to providing the project initiators with invaluable support, such a committee will encourage all members of the school community to consult with one another, take responsibility and get involved.

Awareness-raising and education

In order to achieve the goals of the solidarity ride, the focus must be on awareness-raising and education. The cycling committee could prepare a short presentation to be given to each class. The presentation could focus on:

❧ the concepts behind the greenhouse effect;

❧ the causes and consequences of climate change;

❧ the importance of trees in the fight against climate change;

❧ the problems of deforestation and desertification, especially in the developing countries that the school has decided to help;

- individual and group actions that could be undertaken as concrete steps against climate change;

- the commitment needed from all of Earth's citizens in the fight against climate change;

- solidarity as an effective means of action.

The presentation could end with an introduction to the solidarity ride project and a discussion of the commitment needed from everyone involved in order for the project to succeed. Presentation materials could include tables, graphs, maps, videos and photographs. Let your imagination run wild, but don't forget that excellent educational materials on the subject already exist. There is no need to reinvent the wheel! In most schools, two presenters can cover all the classes, but if the student population is very large, the cycling committee may train some teachers who in turn will give the presentations to their own classes.

Enlist the participation of as many as possible

In a project of this scope, there is no shortage of tasks, such as being part of a first-aid, repair or safety team; helping out the cycling committee; collecting sponsorships; gathering signatures on the petition; or participating as a cyclist. You can recruit volunteers while raising awareness by setting up an interesting booth and inviting all members of the school community to visit you there at noon. This would provide an opportunity to distribute information on the solidarity ride; collect the names of participants; recruit adults to accompany the ride and students to be in charge for the day; collect signatures on the petition for the development of a network of bicycle paths in your municipality; and distribute the sponsor sheet for raising funds.

The size of the event will vary from school to school. It may be wise to limit the number of participants in the first year, and gradually increase it in subsequent years.

Choose a route

The happy band of cyclists that you will form will have a greater impact in the community if you choose a route that is strategic and realistic. Therefore, it is important to:

- choose a route that will give the group the greatest visibility;

- limit the route to 40 or 50 kilometers (25-30 miles) depending on the terrain in your area;

- schedule a stop at a park or school for a lunch break. During the break, put on a show that will energize the cyclists or have a speaker who believes in this cause to give a motivating talk;

Solidarity cyclists petition mayor for a network of bike paths.

- schedule a stop at city hall for the official presentation of the petition to the mayor.

Publicize the event

For the solidarity ride to have the greatest impact, it is important to inform the entire community of the school's commitment to the project. The local media should be made aware of when the ride will take place through a press release. You could also organize a press conference and give each journalist a press kit describing the ride and the spirit of solidarity driving it. The kit could also contain information on climate change, desertification, and the importance of supporting the development of public transit and establishing a network of bicycle routes. Invite journalists to join the cyclists along the route, during the lunch break, or during the official presentation of the petition to the mayor. A team of young reporters can be asked to provide media coverage of the event.

Practical advice for a successful solidarity ride

- Solidarity rides should take place on a school day so that more students and staff are able to participate.

- Arrange for an adequate number of adults to accompany the ride (one adult per 15 students).

- Form teams of students to be responsible for first aid, repairs and safety.

- Ensure that the ride is preceded by a lead car that is clearly identified as part of the ride, and a vehicle to bring up the rear in case of any snags.

- Arrange for a police escort along the entire route.

- Make an appointment with the mayor for an official presentation of the petition on the day of the solidarity ride. Recruit a budding cameraperson to capture this special moment.

- Review the events of the day at the end of the ride.

A solidarity ride definitely requires a large investment of time and energy from the organizing committee, students, teachers and the rest of the school community. However, my experience has shown that in addition to broadening students' scope and view of the world, a solidarity ride allows them to take concrete action that they can be proud of. It provides each of them with the opportunity to take his or her place as an active and responsible citizen.

Happy cycling! ❧

Gilles Bélisle is the coordinator of extracurricular programs at the Jean-Baptiste-Meilleur Secondary School in Repentigny, Québec.

Climate Change Round Table

*By emphasizing consensus rather than winning or losing,
round table discussions help students develop the negotiation skills
needed to implement solutions to climate change*

Level: Grade 5 and up

Objective: Students choose an issue related to climate change and engage in a round table discussion to reach consensus.

Length: Two class periods, one to prepare and one for the round table discussion.

Outcomes

The student will:

❧ recognize that environmental issues are connected to economic, political and social issues;

❧ explain how the round table method of consensus-building attempts to solve problems;

❧ reach a consensus based on negotiation; and

❧ work co-operatively in a group.

Materials: The five stages of round table discussions (see Background below), printed on chart paper.

Background

A round table discussion attempts to create a consensus between several parties. As opposed to a debate, the round table process does not declare winners and losers, but tries to reach a position acceptable to all the parties with the aid of a neutral facilitator. There are five stages:

1. Select an issue.

2. Identify the interest groups (governments, citizens, businesses, etc.) that are affected by the problem in the issue.

3. Interest groups present their position.

4. Negotiate a consensus.

5. Discuss the process.

Since the round table method of decision-making is new to most students, it may be a little difficult at first. It requires the class to work with the utmost cooperation and respect for others and their opinions. Students must get used to discussions in which no one is right or wrong. Review with students that this is not an open fight, but an open discussion. Ban such phrases as

"You're wrong...," "That's a stupid idea...," etc. Instead ask students to say "I don't agree with your idea because...." Spend time explaining a consensus and how to go about reaching it. Emphasize that compromise is essential: all interest groups have to be willing to settle and to give up some of their demands.

The role of the facilitator is key in a successful round table. The facilitator needs to listen carefully, take note of each party's concerns, and move the group towards consensus by focusing on the points that people seem to agree on and letting go of others that present conflict. The teacher should act as the facilitator to keep the discussion on track, at least until students are familiar with the process (see Extension activity).

Procedure

1. Brainstorm or review broad solutions to climate change that may have been covered in previous lessons. These may include:

- discouraging people from driving their cars;
- switching to renewable sources of energy;
- encouraging greater use of public transit and bicycles;
- improving automobile fuel efficiency.

2. For each solution, discuss who must be involved to ensure the success of the solution. For example, increasing the use of more fuel-efficient cars would likely require the participation of engineers, car manufacturers, auto sales companies, government, environmental groups and drivers.

3. Explain that the class will use a method called a round table discussion to discuss an issue related to climate change. Point out the five stages of round table discussions and explain the terms *interest group* (an organization, business or government directly involved in or affected by a problem or issue) and *consensus* (when everyone agrees to something).

4. Have the class choose one of the solutions to global warming that has been discussed and brainstorm some of the practical ways that this solution could be implemented.

Example: If the solution is to discourage driving and encourage the use of public transit, students might come up with the following practical ways to accomplish this:

- increase parking fees in downtown areas;
- require drivers to purchase transit passes as a means of funding local transit;
- increase license plate fees;
- increase funding to the local transit authority;
- reduce fares on local transit.

5. Decide who would be most affected by these measures and divide the class into interest groups accordingly. (For instance, in the example suggested above, the interest groups might be the local transit authority, an environmental group, downtown business owners, and drivers who live in outerlying suburbs.)

6. Ask the interest groups to brainstorm their position on the issue in preparation for presenting it to the class.

7. Seat the groups so they can see one another; for instance, place desks in a large horseshoe with one end open at the front of the class to give the facilitator room to stand and write.

8. Ask each group to present a two-minute summary of their position. The summaries should include both their concerns and the actions that they think need to be taken. The group may elect a spokesperson, but after the first summary, the facilitator may call upon anyone in the group to speak so that each student participates in the round table discussion.

9. The facilitator takes notes on each group's main concerns (i.e., saving money, health, global warming, etc.). Afterwards, the facilitator leads the group through each concern until they reach a consensus on the steps to be taken.

10. The facilitator attempts to find a common ground between all positions: "Are we agreed that...?" Cross out concerns and actions that are controversial. Try to get the class to agree on a few key points. Each group has to agree to at least one concern or action in order to reach the consensus level. (The ideal would be to get the class to agree on what actions need to be taken to resolve this problem.)

11. At the end of the negotiation, the facilitator and the groups attempt to compose a consensus statement.

Closure

After a consensus is reached or time runs out, conduct a group discussion on the process:

Does the round table model work? Why? Why not?
How could it break down?
How could it be improved?
Is this a good way to make decisions?

Extension

Try the jigsaw method in which each student has the opportunity to represent an interest group. In this variation, steps one through six of the procedure remain the same. Students are first divided into interest groups where they brainstorm their position and become "expert" representatives of their group's point of view. While the interest groups are meeting, the teacher can meet with a group of student facilitators — either volunteer or appointed — to review their roles and responsibilities. Round table discussions are then held, with each round table group having one expert from each interest group. It will be interesting to compare the different consensus agreements reached in the small groups. This extension works best if students, especially younger students, have participated in at least one round table discussion with the teacher as facilitator.

This activity is adapted with permission from "Round Table Discussion" in Our Warming Earth: Global Climate Curriculum Unit, Grade 5-6 *by the Toronto Environmental Alliance (see Organizations and Resources section).*

Organizations and Resources

The following lists include Organizations and Other Recommended Resources that can help you to customize your climate change curricula. The organization listings indicate the availability of funding (F), training (T), or teaching resources (R). Where applicable, these resources are listed after the contact information and denoted by (*).

ORGANIZATIONS

CANADA
National Programs

Environment Canada, Inquiry Centre, 351 St. Joseph Boulevard, Hull, QC K1A 0H3, (800) 668-6767, www.ec.gc.ca/cc. **F R**
* *A Matter of Degrees: A Primer on Climate Change; A Change in Our Climate: What's going in our greenhouse?; Canada's Transportation Challenge*

Destination Conservation, Tomorrow Foundation for a Sustainable Future, 10511 Saskatchewan Drive, Edmonton, AB T6E 4S1, (780) 433-8711, www.dc.ab.ca. Partners: (BC) Destination Conservation, (604) 669-6222; (ON) Dearness Environmental Society, (416) 226-6653; (NB) Enerplan Consultants, (506) 858-1300; (NWT) Arctic Energy Alliance, (867) 920-3333; (QC) Earth Values Institute, (450) 658-8614; (SK) Saskatchewan Environmental Society, (306) 665-1915. **T R**

Pembina Institute for Appropriate Development, PO Box 7558, Drayton Valley, AB T7A 1S7, (780) 542-6272 or (613) 235-6288, www.pembina.org, www.climatechangesolutions.com. **T R**
* *Climate Change: Awareness and Action Education Kit* (high school).

The Society, Environment and Energy Development Studies (SEEDS) Foundation, 144 4th Avenue SW S-400, Calgary, AB T2P 3N4, (403) 221-0873, www.greenschools.ca/seeds. **T R**
* *Creating a Climate of Change* (high school video, teacher's kit)

Go for Green, PO Box 450, Station A, Ottawa, ON K1N 6N5, (888) 822-2848, www.goforgreen.ca/asrts. **T R**
* *Active and Safe Routes to School Action Kit* (grades K-8)

Learning for a Sustainable Future, 45 Rideau Street S-303, Ottawa, ON K1N 5W8, (613) 562-2238, www.schoolnet.ca/learning. **T R**

* *Exploring the Issue of Climate Change* (grades 5-8)

Canadian Global Change Program, The Royal Society of Canada, 283 Sparks Street, Ottawa, ON K1R 7X9, (613) 991-6990, www.rsc.ca. **T R**
* *Global Change and Canadians* (with teacher's guide); *Canada and the State of the Planet*

Harmony Foundation, 1183 Fort Street, Victoria, BC V8V 3L1, (250) 380-3001, www.islandnet.com/~harmony. **T R**
* *Climate Change: Community Action Workshop Manual*

Solar Energy Society of Canada, PO Box 33047, Cathedral PO, Regina, SK S4T 7X2, www.solarenergysociety.ca. **R**
* *Canadian Renewable Energy Guide; A Sustainable Energy Future: How do we get there from here?*

Provincial Programs

FEESA, 10506 Jasper Avenue S-1100, Edmonton, AB T5J 2W9, (780) 421-1497, www.feesa.ab.ca. **T R**
* *Climate Change* (poster)

Project WILD, BC Ministry of Environment, Lands and Parks, 300- 1005 Broad Street, Victoria, BC V8W 2A1, (604) 356-7111. **R**
* *Ground Truth Studies Teacher Handbook, Canadian Edition* (high school)

Toronto Environmental Alliance, 30 Duncan Street S 201, Toronto, ON M5V 2C3, (416) 596-0660, www.torontoenvironment.org. **R**
* *Our Warming Earth: Global Climate Change Curriculum Kit for Grades Five and Six*

Scientists and Innovators in the Schools, c/o Centre for Marine Geology, Dalhousie University, Halifax, NS B3H 3J5, (902) 494-2831. **T R**
* *Climate Change Action Packs* (grades 5-10)

UNITED STATES
National Programs

U.S. Environmental Protection Agency (EPA), Information Resources Center, 1200 Pennsylvania Avenue NW MC3404, Washington, DC 20460, (202) 260-5922, www.epa.gov, www.epa.gov/globalwarming. **R**

U.S. Department of Energy, (800) 342-5363, (800) DOE-3237, www.energy.gov, www.energy.gov/issues/climatechange. **R**
* *Get Smart About Energy* (activity CD); *Energy Smart Schools*

National Renewable Energy Laboratory, 1617 Cole Boulevard, Golden, CO 80401-3393, (303) 275-3090, www.nrcl.gov/education. **R**
* *Getting Energized: Learning Activities for 3rd-6th Graders; How to Build a Pizza Box Solar Oven; Solar Energy Science Projects*

National Energy Information Center, EI-3, Energy Information Administration, U.S. Department of Energy, 1000 Independence Avenue SW, Washington, DC 20585, (202) 586-8800, www.eia.doe.gov/bookshelf/eer/kiddietoc.html#table, www.eia.doe.gov/kids. **R**
* *Energy Education Resources K-12; Emissions of Greenhouse Gases in the United States, 1999*

Renewable Energy Policy Project/The Center for Renewable Energy and Sustainable Technology, 1612 K Street NW S-202, Washington, DC 20006, (202) 293-2898, www.repp.org, solstice.crest.org. **R**
* *The Sun's Joules; The On-Line Renewable Energy Education Module Solar For Schools; Educational Uses of The Sun's Joules*

National Energy Education Development Project, 102 Elden Street S-15, Herndon, VA 20170, (800) 875-5029, www.need.org. **T R**

The Alliance to Save Energy, 1200 18th Street NW S-900, Washington, DC 20036, (202) 857-0666, www.ase.org. **T R**
* *Green Schools Program* (energy savings and education); *Update* newsletter

Interstate Renewable Energy Council, PO Box 1156, Latham, NY 12110-1156, (518) 458-6059, www.irecusa.org, www.schoolsgoingsolar.org. **R**
* *Schools Going Solar* (2 volumes); *PV 4 U: Schools Going Solar* electronic newsletter

American Electric Power, Community Relations, 1 Riverside Plaza, Columbus, OH 43215, (614) 223-1668, www.aep.com. **T R**
* *Interactive energy calculator at www.wattsonschools.com; Watts on Schools; Learning from Light; Learning from Wind*

American Solar Energy Society, 2400 Central Avenue Suite G-1, Boulder, CO 80301, (303) 443-3130, www.ases.org. **T R**
* *Science Projects in Renewable Energy and Energy Efficiency*

National Energy Foundation, 3676 California Avenue S-A117, Salt Lake City, UT 84104, (800) 616-8326, www.nef1.org. **T R**
* *Energy Action* (school savings program)

National Science Teachers' Association, 1840 Wilson Boulevard, Arlington, VA 22201-3000, (800) 722-NSTA, www.nsta.org. **R**
* *Forecasting the Future: Exploring the Evidence for Global Climate Change*

Rocky Mountain Institute, 1739 Snowmass Creek Road, Snowmass, CO 81654-9199, (970) 927-3851, www.rmi.org. **R**
* *A Community Energy Workbook: A Guide to Building a Sustainable Economy; Homemade Money: How to Save Energy and Dollars in Your Home*

Aspen Global Change Institute, 100 East Frances Street, Aspen, CO 81611, (303) 925-7376, www.gcrio.org/agci-home.html. **T R**
* *Ground Truth Studies* (high school curriculum); *Earth Pulse NEWS*

Solar Solutions, 1230 East Honey Creek Road, Oregon, IL 61061, (815) 732-7332, www.solarsolutionsseen.com. **T R**
* *Solar Electric Education Kit; Solar Electric Education Network*

Union of Concerned Scientists, 2 Brattle Square, Cambridge, MA 02238-9105, (617) 547-5552, www.ucsusa.org. **R**
* *Renewables Are Ready: A Guide to Teaching Renewable Energy in Junior and Senior High School Classrooms; Confronting Climate Change in California: Ecological Impacts on the Golden State* (curriculum guide)

Institute for Global Environmental Strategies, 1600 Wilson Boulevard S-901, Arlington, VA 22209, (703) 312-0823, www.strategies.org. **F T R**
* *The Potential Consequences of Climate Variability and Change; Earth System Science Education Alliance*

Environmental Defense Fund, 1875 Connecticut Avenue NW, Washington, DC 20009, (800) 684-3322, www.edf.org, www.climatehotmap.org. **R**
* *Global Warming: Understanding the Forecast* (includes book, teacher's manual and video); *Global Warming: Early Warning Signs* (map)

Solar Now, Inc., The Sunroom, 100 Sohier Road, Beverly, MA 01915, (978) 927-9SUN, www.solarnow.org. **T R**
* *Solar Solutions for Schools; Renewable Energy Education Framework*

Enterprise for Education, 1316 3rd St S-103, Santa Monica, CA 90401, (310) 394-9864, www.entfored.com. **R**
* *Electric Car Student Booklet* (grades 7-12); *Teacher's Electric Car Book; The Electric Flyer Model Kit; The Electric Vehicle Classroom Kit; The Greenhouse Effect and Global Warming* (grades 8-11 booklet); *Electricity From Water, Wind and Sunlight* (grades 4-6 kit)

Regional

California Energy Commission, 1516 Ninth Street, Sacramento, CA 95814, www.energy.ca.gov/education. **T R**
* *Energy Quest* (online student resource); *Compendium for Energy Resources* (K-12 curriculum evaluation)

Florida Solar Energy Center, 1679 Clearlake Road, Cocoa, FL 32922-5703, (321) 638-1000, www.fsec.ucf.edu. **T R**
* *Solar Matters* (grades 5-9); *Alternative Fuel Matters* (grades 6-8); *Solar Wonders* (high school)

Center for Energy and Environmental Education, University of Northern Iowa, Cedar Falls, IA 50614-0293, (319) 273-2573, www.uni.edu/ceee. **T R**

Iowa State University, Extension Distribution Center, 119 Kooser Drive, Ames, IA 50011-3171, (515) 294-5247. **R**
* *The Three Little Pigs Investigate Climate Change* (grades 4-8, #4h330a); *Goldilocks and the Three Bears Investigate Climate Change* (grades 4-8, #4h330b); *Issues Investigation Helper/ Leader Guide* (#330ldr)

Gateway Center for Resource Efficiency, Missouri Botanical Garden, 3617 Grandel Square, St. Louis, MO 63108, (314)-577-0220, http://stlouis.missouri. org/gatewaygreening. **T R**

National Center for Appropriate Technology, 3040 Continental Drive, Butte, MT 59702, (406) 494-4572, www.montanagreenpower.com/solar/schools. **R**
* *The Power of Solar Energy: A Curriculum Unit for Grades 7-12*

New Mexico Solar Energy Association, PO Box 8507, Santa Fe, NM 87504, (888) 886-6765, www.NMSEA.org. **R**
* *Energy Pathways: SunChaser2 Curriculum*

North Carolina Solar Center, Box 7401, North Carolina State University, Raleigh, NC 27695-7401, (919) 515-3480, www.ncsc.ncsu.edu/eduprog.htm. **T R**

Northeast Sustainable Energy Association, 50 Miles Street, Greenfield, MA 01301, (413) 774-6051, www.nesea.org. **T R**
* *Getting Around Without Gasoline* (grades 5-9); *Getting Around Clean and Green* (grades 5-9); *Choose Your Future Adventure Game* (grades 4-7); *Cars of Tomorrow and the American Community* (high school unit); *Totally TREE-Mendous Activities* (grades 4-7); *Future Wheels for a Sustainable America* (resource list); *Trip Tally: Discovering Environmental Solutions* (grades 3-6); *Travel Solutions to Global Warming* (grade 5); *Junior Solar Sprint* (video)

Ohio Energy Project, 7099 Huntley Road S-105A, Columbus, OH 43229, (614) 785-1717, www.ohioenergy.org. **T R**
* *Energy Bike* program; *Ohio's Energy Smart Schools* program; *Kids Teaching Kids* workshops; *Youth Energy Summits* (grades 7-12)

Wisconsin K-12 Energy Education Program (KEEP), WCEE, University of Wisconsin-Stevens Point, Stevens Point, WI 54481, (715) 346-4163, www.energyed.ecw.org. **T R**
* *A Conceptual Guide to K-12 Energy Education; Energy Education Activity Guide; Know the Flow of Energy in Your School; Promising Energy Education Practices; KEEP Going* (newsletter)

OTHER RECOMMENDED CURRICULA & RESOURCES

Alvord, Katie. *Divorce Your Car! Ending the Love Affair with the Automobile*. Gabriola Island, BC: New Society Publishers, 2000, ISBN 0-86571-408-8, (800) 567-6772.

Climate Change Calculator (online), University of British Columbia, Vancouver, (604) 822-8198, www.climcalc.net.

Dauncey, Guy. *Stormy Weather: 101 Solutions to Global Change*. Gabriola Island, BC: New Society Publishers, 2001, ISBN 0-86571-421-5, (800) 567-6772, www.newsociety.com.

the Earth changes! (video, high school). the Earth Changes!, PO Box 187, Station B, Montreal, QC H3B 3J7, (514) 989-2154.

Engwicht, David. *A Bit of This and A Bit of That* (video); *The Art of Placemaking* (video); *Reclaiming Our*

Cities and Towns: Better Living with Less Traffic. David Engwicht Communications, 658 Shale City Road, Ashland, OR 97520, www.lesstraffic.com.

————. *Street Reclaiming: Creating Livable Streets and Vibrant Communities.* Gabriola Island, BC: New Society Publishers, 1999, ISBN 0-86571-404-5, (800) 567-6772, www.newsociety.com.

Environmental Action: Energy Conservation, teacher's guide (ISBN 0-20149-528-7) and student edition (ISBN 0-20149-529-5). Menlo Park, CA: Dale Seymour Publications, 1998, Orders: (USA) Dale Seymour Publications, (800) 872-1100; (Canada) Addison-Wesley, (800) 387-8028.

Hocking, Colin, Cary I. Sneider, John Erickson and Richard Golden. *Global Warming and the Greenhouse Effect* (grades 7-8). Berkeley CA: GEMS, Lawrence Hall of Science, 1990, ISBN 0-91251-175-3. Orders: (USA) (510) 642-7771, (Canada) Addison-Wesley, (800) 387-8028.

Kaufman, A. *Exploring Solar Energy: Principles and Projects*, 1989 (ISBN 0-91116-860-5, grades 7-12); and *Exploring Solar Energy II: Activities in Solar Electricity*, 1995 (ISBN 0-91116-889-3, grades 7-12). Ann Arbor: Prakken Publications, (800) 530-9673, www.techdirections.com.

Kindred, Merle. *Sunshine is Free* (grades K-3); *Sun Power* (grades 4-6), 1998. Merle Kindred, 1016 Crestwood Drive, Hancock, MI 49930-1135, (906) 482-7803.

MediCinema. *Energy, The Pulse of Life; Energy Choices* (videos and teacher's guides). MediCinema Ltd., 131 Albany Avenue, Toronto, ON M5R 3C5 (416) 977-0569.

National 4H Council. *Making Choices, Going Places: Transportation and The Environment* (grades 9-12 curriculum), 1999. National 4-H Council, 7100 Connecticut Avenue, Chevy Chase, MD 20815-4999, (301) 961-2800.

The NoodleHead Network. *Simple Things You Can Do To Save Energy In Your School* (video and activity guide, grades 4-8); *Simple Things You Can Do To Save Energy: The Power is in Your Hands* (video and home energy audit, grades 3-8). Burlington, VT: The NoodleHead Network, (800) 639-5680, www.noodlehead.com.

Radabaugh, Joseph. *Heaven's Flame: A Guide to Solar Cookers.* Ashland, OR: Home Power Publishing, 1998, ISBN 0-96295-882-4, (541) 512-0201, www.homepower.com.

Sussman, Art. *Dr. Art's Guide to Planet Earth*, 2000, ISBN 1-89013-273-X. (USA) Chelsea Green Publishing Company, (800) 639-4099; (Canada) Nimbus Publishing, (800) 646-2879.

Woelfle, Gretchen. *The Wind at Work: An Activity Guide to Windmills.* Chicago: Independent Publishers Group/Chicago Review Press, 1997, ISBN 1-55652-308-4, (312) 337-0747.

Curriculum Index

Subject	Grades K-3	Grades 4-6	Grades 7-8	Grades 9-12
Art	30, 33, 38	30, 33, 36, 56, 66	33, 36, 56, 66, 68	31, 36, 56, 66, 68
Health / Physical Education	32-34	32-34, 35-36, 40	32-34, 35-36, 40, 61-63	32-34, 35-36, 40, 44-48, 61-63
Home Economics			17-19, 25-27, 59-60, 61-63, 69-70	17-19, 25-27, 55, 59-60, 61-63, 69-70
Language Arts	30, 33, 38	28, 30, 33, 38, 66	28, 31, 33, 39, 66, 68, 69-70	28, 31, 46-47, 66, 68, 69-70
Mathematics	30, 33	28, 33, 54, 59-60	28, 31, 33, 38, 41, 54, 57, 59-60, 66	28, 31, 33, 39, 41, 45-48, 54, 57, 59-60, 66
Music	33	33		
Science	11-12, 17-19, 30, 54	6-8, 11-13, 15-16, 17-19, 22-24, 25-27, 28, 54-55, 58, 60-61	6-8, 11-13, 15-16, 17-19, 22-24, 25-27, 28, 31, 33, 38, 54-55, 58, 59-60, 66	6-8, 11-13, 15-16, 17-19, 22-24, 28, 31, 33, 36, 44-48, 49-52, 54-55, 58, 66
Social Studies	17-19, 20-21, 38	7-8, 17-19, 27, 28, 38, 55, 58, 69-70	6-8, 16, 17-19, 27, 28, 31, 36, 38, 55, 58, 66, 69-70	6-8, 16, 17-19, 28, 31, 36, 39, 44-48, 49-52, 55, 58, 66, 69-70

Index

Green Teacher

Education for Planet Earth

A quarterly magazine by and for educators, *Green Teacher* provides inspiration, ideas and classroom-ready materials to enhance environmental and global education across the curriculum at all grade levels. Some of the themes covered since 1991 include:

waste reduction ✷ urban forestry
environmental monitoring ✷ sustainability
nature awareness ✷ waterways rehabilitation
humane education ✷ ecological footprints
transportation alternatives ✷ biodiversity
human rights ✷ peace education
sustainable agriculture ✷ climate change
habitat protection ✷ marine ecosystems

E-Packs: Collections of the Best of *Green Teacher*

E-Packs are collections of articles, delivered by e-mail, which contain some of the best of the curriculum ideas, perspectives and activities published in past issues of *Green Teacher* magazine:

✷ Green Teacher's Greatest Hits I & II, Transforming Schoolyards I & II,
✷ Science/Technology K-6 & 7-12, Social/Multicultural Studies K-6 & 7-12,
✷ Integrated High School Curriculum I & II, Language Arts/Art K-6 & 7-12.

Other Books by Green Teacher

Greening School Grounds: Creating Habitats for Learning
Des idées fraîches à l'école: Activités et projets pour contrer les changements climatiques

For more information,
please call (416) 960-1244 or visit our web site at
www.greenteacher.com